Chak

The Practical Guide to Awakening and
Balancing Chakras for Beginners to Feel
Great and Radiate Positive Energy using
Self Healing Techniques

Judith Yandell

© Copyright 2020 Judith Yandell - All rights reserved.

The content contained within this book may not be reproduced, duplicated or transmitted without direct written permission from the author or the publisher.

Under no circumstances will any blame or legal responsibility be held against the publisher, or author, for any damages, reparation, or monetary loss due to the information contained within this book, either directly or indirectly.

Legal Notice:

This book is copyright protected. It is only for personal use. You cannot amend, distribute, sell, use, quote or paraphrase any part, or the content within this book, without the consent of the author or publisher.

Disclaimer Notice:

Please note the information contained within this document is for educational and entertainment purposes only. All effort has been executed to present accurate, up to date, reliable, complete information. No warranties of any kind are declared or implied. Readers acknowledge that the author is not engaged in the rendering of legal, financial, medical or professional advice. The content within this book has been derived from various sources. Please consult a licensed professional before attempting any techniques outlined in this book.

By reading this document, the reader agrees that under no circumstances is the author responsible for any losses, direct or indirect, that are incurred as a result of the use of the information contained within this document, including, but not limited to, errors, omissions, or inaccuracies.

TABLE OF CONTENTS

Introduction

Yet another sleepless night before your alarm for work blares in your ear, forcing you to get up and drag yourself to the shower. Shocker, there was a power cut during the night and now the water is ice cold. Tired, annoyed, and now cold, you rush down stairs to make yourself something to eat before heading out to work. The power cut tripped your entire electrical system, nothing is working. You weigh your options of fixing the problem yourself or getting a professional to do it when you realize the time on your phone does not match what is on the kitchen clock. You are late! You grab what you can and rush to work, only to be caught in the morning traffic. You say to yourself that this was a slight hiccup in your day, it can't dictate how the rest of day goes. Can it?

You sit down at your desk and start getting to work. There is a tickle at the back of your throat. Clearing your throat multiple times has your coworkers looking at you with distrust. If you are sick, they do not want to be infected. Their distrust is almost palpable and you try your best to stick it out but soon, that call to the boss's office appears in your inbox. Sighing, you get to your feet and go to see the head honcho. There is no smile. How can you be sick for the third time this month? Three times? You hadn't noticed and thought back to earlier in the month. There was that stomach thing a week back, a nasty migraine the week before that, and the month isn't done yet. The boss suggests it is time to take a holiday, but you are forced to bring up the huge project that you are working on. You leave the office with an order to get some vitamins and do overtime to complete the project on time.

It is dark by the time you get home and you are exhausted. You arrive at a dark, cold house and you realize you forgot to call anyone to fix the problem with your power. It is way too late now. Your options for dinner are either leftover pizza or whatever is growing in the back of your fridge. Your stomach moans in protest and you decide instead to crawl into bed defeated, only to repeat this process again in the morning.

Does this sound like your life? Forgetfulness? Unexplained illnesses? Everyone citing that it's stress or not getting enough rest? Don't rush to your computer to look for answers on the internet, heaven knows what that may tell you! What if I told you that inside your body, there are spiritual energies at work that are trying to help you, but things in your life are blocking them from doing their jobs? With this book, I am pleased to invite you to the wonderful world of chakras to help you improve your own well-being.

Chapter 1:
Chakras: An Overview

Spiritual energy? Chakras? What are you on about? How can this be a replacement for doctor's advice? Let it be said that you cannot replace doctor's advice with the information received from this book. The information here is just a guide to living to your full potential in harmony with your own internal energies. What are those energies? Well, before that can be answered, you need to understand where all this came from. So, let's delve into a good old fashion history lesson.

History of Chakras

The earliest mention of chakras (cakra), meaning wheel or disk, can be found in the Sanskrit texts called Vedus texts (The Editors of Encyclopaedia

Britannica, n.d.) somewhere between 1500-500 BC. It made reference to who we are as living organisms, which are made up of two parts, one which is the physical body (sthula sarira), and the other, which is made of energy known as the subtle body (sukshma sarira) (Sharma, 2006). It is also believed that these two parts need to work together to lead a healthy life (Lochtefeld, 2002). This leads to the thought that the mind and body affect one another. Thus, a healthy mind equals a healthy body and vice versa.

For a moment, consider how your blood moves through your body. There are channels that your blood moves through called arteries and veins. These channels take your blood through your entire body, feeding it the nutrients and oxygen it needs, which leads to a healthy body. This is for your physical body —what about your non-physical one? It is actually very similar. Instead of blood, arteries, veins, and organs, you have energy, which travels along energy channels called nadi to nodes (areas) called chakras (Lochtefeld, 2002). Though many chakras exist in the body (some say well over several thousand) this book is going to concentrate on the seven main chakras identified by Hinduism (Lochtefeld, 2002; The Editors of Encyclopaedia Britannica, n.d). Each of these chakras are unique and can be identified by different colors, shapes, locations, natural elements, number of lotus petals, etc.

The concept of a physical body and a non-physical body (mind and/or spirit) is not an alien concept and can be found amongst many cultures and eras (Samuel & Johnston, 2013), but where does that leave us in our modern society?

Where Does It Leave Us in Modern Times?

The modern world seems so much better than what it was thousands of years ago. We have good medicine, better transport methods, and we mostly live much longer lives. However, a good saying comes to mind: All that glitters is not gold. Though our lives have improved physically, we have traded something away that is more precious than anything else. What is that? Time.

Our lives have gotten so busy with work, families, and trying to find some time to just take a breather that we don't take care of ourselves. Obesity, heart disease, migraines, and a multitude of other illnesses proves that we do not have time to look after ourselves physically, much less trying to look at our inner energies.

A good example comes from something as simple as making a cup of tea. Anyone who is a tea enthusiast will know that each type of tea has its own technique when it comes to brewing time, the temperature of the water, or even what container is used for brewing in or drinking from. Next time you buy some tea, look at the instructions and you will see that most tea takes about five minutes maximum before you can enjoy your beverage. This time can vary depending on how you like your tea made, and if you like to drink it piping hot, or prefer it a little cooler.

Five minutes. Can you truly relax spending just five minutes making yourself a hot beverage? If you can, fantastic! However, most of us need significantly more time before we feel remotely relaxed. Now, think of the traditional Chinese and Japanese tea ceremonies. Do these take five minutes? No, they can last anywhere from an hour to four hours! Imagine being able to relax for four hours! Most of us can't. Could you spare 30 minutes? Maybe? Great! You only need a few moments out of your day to look into your own inner energies. Now, what exactly is there to look at?

The Seven Chakras

In this book we will concentrate on the seven main chakras, which can be found along the spinal cord in different locations, from above your head to the base of your spine (Lochtefeld, 2002; Jones & Ryan, 2006). To help with finding the different chakras, it is suggested that you find a nice comfortable place to sit. Though not necessary, a nice quiet area can help you concentrate on what you are trying to find. When in doubt, note Figure 1 to help you in locating your own chakras.

Fig 1. Chakras.

First let's find the Root chakra. This chakra can be found close to the coccyx (tail bone), and its energy channels move towards your belly.

Next is the Sacral chakra. This node is easy to find. Place a hand just below your belly button and you will be over it. This chakra's energy channels move upwards towards the next chakra.

Then we have the Solar Plexus chakra. This is pretty much self-explanatory. The place where your lower ribs join to your breastbone is where this chakra

17

makes its home. Its energy channels move up towards your heart.

The next chakra is called the Heart chakra for an obvious reason. It is found over your heart, close to the center of the breastbone. This chakra connects both the higher and the lower chakra with energy channels that move down towards the Solar Plexus chakra and up towards the throat.

We follow up with the Throat chakra. For this chakra, lightly touch the area above where your collarbones join. Do this gently! You will choke if you press too hard. This chakra's energy channels move down towards the Heart chakra and up towards the area between your eyes.

You may have heard of the next chakra in the past because of popular media. This is the Third Eye and it can be found between your eyes. The energy channels run down towards your throat and extend up beyond your head.

Last, but by no means least, is the Crown chakra. This is not directly part of your body, but rather is just slightly above your head. This chakra's energy channels flow down towards your face as well as up into the universe.

Although the chakras mentioned are located on the torso, it is not the only place where we can access them. Later in this book, we will talk about how they can be accessed through our hands and our feet with the use of reflexology. However, before we can move onto that, we need to discuss each chakra in depth so that there is a clear understanding as to what each one represents to us.

The First Chakra: Root Chakra

The Root chakra, also known as *Muladhara* (Mindvalley, 2017), meaning root and support, is the node that is closely associated with your physical survival on this planet. Survival can mean many different things for people—though in modern times, having a roof over your head with enough to eat is considered survival. This chakra is represented by the color red, the element of earth, and a lotus with four petals (Grimes, 1996).

When this chakra is in its balanced state, your mind is at peace when you think about things you need to survive, be that money, shelter, or caring for someone else's survival (Mindvalley, 2017).

The Second Chakra: Sacral Chakra

The Sacral chakra, *Svadhishana* (Mindvalley, 2017), meaning place of self or where one's self is established, is associated with your own identity and creative energy. This chakra motivates you to enjoy all that life has to offer you but warns of overindulgence during your physical existence. It is represented by the color orange, the element of water, and a six petaled lotus (Grimes, 1996).

When this chakra is balanced, you will find that you are able to enjoy all that life has to offer in terms of pleasure, be that food, love, or intimacy, without overindulging (Mindvalley, 2017).

The Third Chakra: Solar Plexus Chakra

The Solar Plexus chakra, *Manipura* (Mindvalley, 2017), meaning lustrous gem, is the node associated with your own internal self-confidence and "gut feelings." You know the feeling you get when you walk alone in the dark, in an unfamiliar place? The feeling that warns you of potential danger about places and people? You can thank this chakra for those warnings. It offers wisdom and the ability to make quick decisions when you find yourself in situations that could be dangerous. It is represented by the color yellow, the element of fire, and a 10 petaled lotus (Grimes, 1996).

When this chakra is in balance, you will find that you are able to make clear, decisive plans and put them into action without panicked thoughts (Mindvalley, 2017). You are as cool as a cucumber. So next time you get that funny feeling in the pit of your stomach that something is wrong, leave. You are being told this for a reason.

The Fourth Chakra: Heart Chakra

The Heart chakra, *Anahata* (Mindvalley, 2017), meaning unhurt or unstruck, is the node associated with quite a few things. First is the obvious one, love, but not just love for others but also love for yourself, something most people are unable to do. Then there is compassion, again, for you and others. Finally, it is also associated with your health and healing. This chakra is represented by the color green, the element of air, and 12 lotus petals (Grimes, 1996).

When this chakra is balanced you find that you are able to love yourself as much as those around you, even though your situation may be a difficult one. Remember, being kind to another human being costs you nothing, but could mean the world to the one that receives that kindness (Mindvalley, 2017).

The Fifth Chakra: Throat Chakra

The Throat chakra, *Vishuddha* (Mindvalley, 2017), meaning purest or very pure, is the node associated with being able to speak up about personal truths and finding the courage to do so. Due to the location of this chakra, what you speak is heavily linked to your heart. So be sure of your own feelings before you speak. Words hold many meanings, as harmful as what they can be, they can also be spoken with love and encouragement to others. This node is associated with the color blue, the element of space, and a 16 petaled lotus (Grimes, 1996).

When this chakra is balanced you find yourself able to communicate feelings of love and kindness to others and yourself with ease. You also find the courage to speak the truths about yourself (Mindvalley, 2017). A good example of this is where you are able to talk about your own achievements with a sense of pride and not hide your feelings about it.

The Sixth Chakra: Third Eye Chakra

The Third Eye chakra, *Anja* (Agya) (Mindvalley, 2017), means beyond wisdom. The Third Eye is not a concept that is limited to chakras but is often seen in multimedia where it often hints towards a psychic nature. Though not everyone can see into the future, this chakra is associated with extrasensory perception. That means you are able to sense something that is beyond your normal senses. Often called intuition, it is akin to your gut feeling. This chakra is associated with the color indigo, and a lotus flower with only two petals.

When this chakra is balanced you are able to receive messages that are both from the physical world, from your five senses, as well as messages from the world of energy (Mindvalley, 2017). You are able to receive these messages and just know things, and will not be concerned as to why you know these things.

The Seventh Chakra: Crown

The Crown chakra, *Sahaswara* (Sahastrar) (Mindvalley, 2017), meaning thousand petaled, is a rather interesting chakra, as it is not directly connected to your body but rather, is found slightly above your head. This chakra allows you to interact with the rest of the universe around you and allows for you to achieve your personal goals. This chakra is represented by a lotus with a thousand petals and the colors associated with it can be violet to multicolored.

Once this chakra is balanced all other chakras will align (Mindvalley, 2017). Sounds easy, right? Nope. This is the hardest of the chakras to balance and requires a lot of work on your part to achieve. However, once this chakra is balanced, it is akin to being one with the universe, where you are your consciousness and you can interact with the vast universe on that level.

Visualizing Your Own Chakras

Now that you know more about the seven chakras, let's take a moment to visualize them in turn. Are you still sitting in that comfortable position? Excellent, then we can move on to visualizing these nodes. You may need some uninterrupted time to do the next activity so if you are not comfortable, find a place where you could sit in silence for a few uninterrupted minutes.

Comfortable? Good, we can begin. Each chakra has been assigned a color and this will allow you to visualize them more easily. Starting with the chakra that roots us to the physical world, picture a spinning red disc that pushes energy upwards. This is your Root chakra. The energy flows as you breathe, so don't forget to do this as you relax. Follow the flow of energy to your next chakra. Do you remember the next color? That's right, orange; feel it pulsing and spinning just under your belly button, coaxing energy even higher. That was your Sacral chakra. Move a little higher with your flowing energy to see a spinning yellow disk just under your ribs. You should be familiar with this part of your body. You often feel emotions here. The energy is still moving up, so follow it to the spinning green disk upon your breastbone, close to your heart. The Heart chakra is often physically touched by our hands when we are deeply moved by the actions and words of others. It may even bring a smile to your face when these events happen. With this chakra you will feel the pull of the energy channels both downwards as well as upwards. If you feel you are ready to continue, then follow the flow of energy upwards. However, if you feel you haven't connected with the first three chakras before this one, relax and flow backwards to start again. There is no rush to accomplish this immediately, remember, we are taking the time to get to know our innermost powers, it does take time. Think of it as meeting a stranger and getting to know them better.

If you are ready to continue, flow up towards the next chakra. Here you find a beautiful blue disk spinning. If you are struggling to find it, hum a little tune and place your fingers just above where your collarbones join. You should be able to feel the vibrations under your fingers. This is your Throat chakra. Once more, the energy channels run up and down. The Heart chakra and Throat chakra are in areas of our body that we are very familiar with, so spend some time here if you find a lot of comfort. Only move up the energy channel if you are ready to do so.

The next two chakras have more to do with the immaterial-plane (energy plane), so don't be nervous if you find your connection to their nodes are a little more difficult to obtain. You need to be a little more open minded to experience them to their fullest.

Follow the energy channels from the throat up to between your eyes. Here you can find a disk of indigo spinning—this is your Third Eye chakra. Spend some time getting to know this chakra and the feelings that may come from it. Once more, the energy channels move both up and down. You decide where you wish to go next. The final journey takes you outside of your body, a few inches above your head. If you have trouble visualizing this, put your hand on your head, the Crown will be resting on top of your hand. It is a beautiful disk that spins, showing many different colors varying from white to a deep purple. Here you will feel two different pulls. One will be back into your body towards your Third Eye chakra, and the other upwards to join the universe. If you are able to connect to this chakra you will find yourself at peace with yourself and the universe around you.

Were you able to find all your chakras? Were some a little more difficult to visualize than others? Sometimes events in our lives can cause these nodes to become overactive or blocked, pretty much like what can happen to our arteries or veins when they become blocked with plaque. We know what can happen to our physical body when this occurs. We could suffer heart attacks or strokes, which can leave our body in a debilitated state or worse. However, when we look at our immaterial body, how can it be affected by the nodes becoming overactive or completely blocked? Remember that our immaterial body and our physical body is joined. What affects the one, affects the other. In the next chapter, we will discuss the causes of the imbalance in the chakras and how this can affect both the immaterial and the physical body.

Chapter 2:
Imbalance

Balance is very important. Think about what happens to us when balance is lost. Family life is disrupted, interpersonal relationships can crumble, and we can lose that dreaded battle with the scale. Bringing balance to our physical lives is tough enough as it is without thinking about how to bring balance to our own internal energies. However, this needs to be done. You may ask, 'Why?' The physical body is influenced by the immaterial body (Lochtefeld, 2002). Think about that diet you keep failing to stick to because you just *had* to snack on that cupcake, or enjoy that night out with your friends and you enjoyed one too many alcoholic drinks. You just couldn't resist the temptation. If your diet is balanced, you shouldn't have cravings and you should be able to limit yourself on treats, but something is stopping you. So if it is not physical, then it needs to be something else. We look to the chakras to reveal the answers. Chakras don't just exist in perfect harmony; they are influenced by many things and may suffer because of them. In this chapter, we aim to identify warning signs that scream that something is out of balance in your life and can be fixed by simply needing a holiday or needing to book an appointment with your physician.

Warning Signs

As discussed earlier, we know that the chakras act as nodes, which energy channels move through to move energy from the lower plane (physical realm) to the higher plane (non-physical realm) (The Editors of Encyclopaedia Britannica, n.d.). That energy is meant to move as water does down a river. If water is halted in its movement, it will remain standing and can become stagnant. This water is considered unhealthy and should not be consumed, but what about energy that is halted? Our body's natural energy can be halted by chakras that become blocked. Each chakra is different in the symptoms (physical, spiritual, or even emotional) caused by a blockage or being under or overactive (Patel, 2020). According to Schmidt (2019) there are five warning signs that could mean that your chakras are out of balance. The first is that you do not feel yourself and something is just 'off,' you can't explain it in words but you do not feel right. The second is that you get sick. Everyone gets sick from time to time and we shrug it off more often than not, but then the third warning sign happens. You are sick again, possibly soon after recovering from your initial illness. The fourth warning sign is that you are making mistakes you would not usually make, or you are making mistakes more often than you usually do. At this point you must be thinking that you need a vacation, and most people will take a break but not everyone does. Some people like to push through because as humans, we are quite a stubborn species. That is when the final warning sign raises its head. You are left with the feeling that the world is going to end as things seem to be falling apart around you. At this point, you are overwhelmed, terrified, don't know where to turn, and feel like you are drowning. It is time to step back and evaluate your life. Is this a physical problem or is it perhaps a deeper problem? Though this book cannot help you directly with problems at work, it can help identify which chakra is causing you the problems.

Influences of Blocked Chakras on the Body

According to Patel (2020) and Mindvalley (2017), there are many problems that are caused by chakras that are not functioning as they should. Chakras can be blocked by various internal and external things and become underactive. When this occurs, the other chakras need to start working harder and can become overactive. Thus, it takes only a single chakra to be out of balance to cause the others to fall out of alignment. Below, the most common ailments will be listed for each chakra and will be divided into symptoms of overactive or underactive. The treatment will differ depending on which phase the chakra is in.

Root Chakra

When every aspect of your physical survival (food, shelter, money) is met, your Root chakra can become underactive and you can become too relaxed with your surroundings. Symptoms can include excessive daydreaming and a lowered ability to concentrate on things that are important. People may say you have your head in the clouds and you need to come back down to earth.

An overactive Root chakra is not so laid back as it is screaming at you that your survival is in jeopardy even though nothing is wrong. Your anxiety is through the roof for no reason and this can cause you to tense up. You are constantly worried about where your next paycheck will come from. Problems associated with this are ailments from the location of the Root chakra downwards. In men there are prostate problems, in women it is ovarian cyst; both genders have problems in their legs, knees, and feet. Even lower back pain and lower digestive problems have been noted. Because of the digestion problems, there could be some eating disorders that come to light and this can affect your immune system.

Sacral Chakra

The Sacral chakra energy is one of creativity and passion. When we spend a lot of time on a project (work or pleasure) and do not enjoy our accomplishments, we cause this chakra to become underactive. Once underactive, we lose our drive to do anything we once enjoyed, leading to depression, lowered sex drive, impotence (both in the bedroom and out of it), and losing the passion we had to do anything creative. Other symptoms that have been noted include urinary tract problems, lower back, hip, and pelvic pain. Emotional issues that arrive include being unable to express emotions on what we want and having a constant fear of being betrayed by those we love.

An overactive Sacral chakra is something many people battle with. One word: overindulgence. There are many things that give us pleasure (food, love, etc.) and though we should enjoy all that we can, it needs to be done in moderation, especially when it comes to things that are not really that good for you. An overactive Sacral chakra can lead to obesity, addiction, and hormonal imbalances that cause us to become restless with ourselves.

Solar Plexus Chakra

The Solar Plexus chakra is one of self-confidence. When you are confident in what you do, you are in charge of all aspects of your life. If that control were to be taken away from you for any reason, your Solar Plexus chakra will become underactive. With the loss of control over your own life, you could become indecisive and insecure about everything. You will second guess yourself, becoming timid and maybe seeking reassurance to try and gain your confidence back. This will make you appear needy and annoying to those around you. Emotionally, you become your own worst enemy. Your inner critic is telling you that you are a failure and you shouldn't bother trying and you become terrified of any kind of rejection. Because you are constantly trying to get the reassurance that you crave, you often feel fatigued and are unable to get the energy to continue.

As bad as an underactive Solar Plexus chakra can be, it is even worse when it is overactive. The control you enjoy in your own life now starts to bleed out and you find yourself wanting to control those around you. This leads to micromanaging the people in your life as YOU need that control, causing you to lose empathy and compassion with them. No one likes to be micromanaged. Friendships will be affected by this. Physical problems that can occur include digestive, gallbladder, pancreas, kidney, and appendix (if you still have yours) problems.

Heart Chakra

The Heart chakra is a very important chakra, as it is the node that has energy moving up towards the Crown chakra as well as back down towards the Root chakra. Not only that, but it is also the chakra that is in control of all our emotions. Unbalance here can be seen in our emotional state as well as our physical being. An underactive Heart chakra causes you to have problems in making connections with other people. You guard your heart jealously against potential hurt and refuse to let anyone in, friends or lovers. You feel out of touch with yourself, unable to show any love for anything. Physical issues that arise are generally circulation issues. Imagine cold feet as a metaphor for a cold heart. You may even feel that you will never find love and will always be alone.

An overactive Heart chakra is a lot less guarded and causes a person to lose personal boundaries in all aspects of their life. This can manifest in many ways; making terrible choices all in the name of love, putting others' welfare ahead of yours to your own detriment, overbearing to the point of suffocation, all of which can lead to interpersonal issues with those around you. You may even feel jealousy and bitterness when your overbearing feelings are not met with what you demand from those around you. Physical problems noted here mostly concentrate on your chest area including, but not limited to, asthma, heartburn, increased heart rate, palpitations, and pain to the upper back, shoulders, all the way down to the wrists. That is what you get for holding onto all that emotion. Share but only to a point. Not every person can accept or give the love you have.

Throat Chakra

The Throat chakra is where our physical voice comes from. If you are someone who loves to tell stories, you know what it is like to be interrupted, spoken over, ignored, or one-upped by people around you. An underactive Throat chakra is caused when we decide to remain silent instead of completing what we wanted to say. If this happens often enough, you will likely become too shy to talk, afraid of the interruption that could potentially occur. This leads to problems expressing one's self. Holding one's tongue or swallowing back unspoken words causes the energy, meant to be spoken, to become stale and can lead to digestive problems. Most other physical problems that occur include many problems in the throat in forms of thyroid problems and soreness. Instances of sore ears are also noted.

An overactive Throat chakra causes you to try too hard to be heard amongst people, especially when you feel ignored. This leads to a raised voice and even interrupting people who were in the middle of a conversation. This tends to brand you as someone who is overly talkative or someone who likes the sound of their own voice. Physical issues that occur here are mostly found in the mouth with ulcers, cavities, and infections to the mouth and throat.

Third Eye Chakra

The Third Eye chakra is where we get our intuitive feelings, where the body just knows something without knowing why it knows things. The imbalance in this chakra can be quite varied in its nature. An underactive Third Eye chakra is quite common amongst people, as few give credence to someone who just knows something and can't offer proof as to how they came to a certain conclusion. Think of the time you pointed out to someone in your life that you felt a person they were with was wrong for them. How did they react? Did they just accept what you said? Or did they immediately bombard you with questions as to why you know this or even accuse you of being jealous? Likely the latter event happened. You pull back, not willing to start a fight because you have no proof, only a feeling. Then, after some time, something happens and your friend comes to realize that you were right but are they grateful? Not usually, because they think you may have sabotaged them in some way. Another possibility is that you have that intuitive feeling but you don't act on it and your friend gets hurt, and you are left feeling guilty, thinking: If I had only spoken up! Because of this, we tend to ignore these feelings, brushing them off and holding our tongues when we really shouldn't. When you deny these feelings you are actually preventing the flow of energy to your Third Eye, which in turn prevents us from connecting to the immaterial realm via our Crown chakra. Physical problems that can occur are focused around the eyes including headaches, eye strain, blurred vision, allergies, and other sinus problems.

After reading all that you must be thinking: If this is what happens when the Third Eye chakra is underactive, what is it like when it is over active? Luckily, it is fairly rare and not nearly as bad, but it does lead to obsession with the immaterial realm. Well that doesn't sound so bad. What is the problem? The problem is that whilst you are immersed in activities like ghost hunting, tarot card reading, and divining, you are missing out on all the experiences that make us human and not enjoying the physical realm. Physical problems that can occur is mostly to do with our attitudes; things like moodiness and stubbornness.

Crown Chakra

The Crown chakra is the node that connects us to the immaterial universe, where our energy can join with the energy of all other things. Luckily for us, this chakra can only be imbalanced in one way and there is very little you can actually do about it. An underactive Crown chakra simply means that you are human. Like the rest of us. You are well aware of the physical world but aren't really in touch with the immaterial world. This chakra is very difficult to align but if you have aligned all your other chakras this node usually realigns, allowing you to enjoy your own personal energy, as well as the consciousness energy that the immaterial world is made up of. There are some physical problems that can occur when this chakra is underactive, these can include rigid thinking, paralysis in thoughts when trying to analyze a situation, as well as the constant fear of being alienated by people around you.

But what about an overactive Crown chakra? All the other chakras can be overactive. Why can't the Crown chakra be overactive? Simple, the universe's energy is boundless. You cannot cause it to explode by adding your own consciousness to it. Don't worry too much about it.

Am I Broken?

"So if my chakras are unbalanced is there something wrong with me?" The simple answer is no. We all go through different things at different times during our lives. Some people handle them well whilst others need a little more help. Some people almost instinctively know how to 'fix' themselves when they feel that their life is unbalanced (reading a book, painting, taking a walk, etc.) but not everyone has this skill. Sometimes, this is learned through trial and error, other times they are told what is needed to help them feel better.

An unbalanced chakra is not a damaged chakra. This is important to remember. Whilst you are alive and breathing your chakras exist in one form or another (over or underactive). They do not need to be 'fixed'; they are not broken. They just need to be realigned so that your life can get back on track.

"Is this easy? Expensive?" Well, that is up to you. How much time and money are you willing to spend on yourself? If you get the same feeling of joy and relaxation from taking a thirty-minute walk compared to a two week cruise, then you need to think which is easier for you to do.

"Can I realign my own chakras or do I need a professional?" Again, that is up to you. This book seeks to educate you about what you can do for yourself, but if you find that you are unable to do it there are professionals that can help.

"I have had these problems all my life. Why should I bother with aligning my chakras?" Well, do you want the problems to continue to your dying breath or even be the cause of it? Realigning chakras may not extend your life to immortality, but they will give you peace and make you feel like your life is mostly, if not completely in order. Feeling relaxed and stress-free is something we should all strive towards.

As the following chapter will show; aligning chakras is not difficult or expensive to do. What do you really have to lose except some time?

Chapter 3:
Bring Balance to Your Inner-Self

Everything in nature has a delicate balance. You will never see more wolves than there are deer. If you do, then you know that the balance has been disturbed by something and eventually, nature will correct this imbalance. Sometimes it is people removing the wolves from the area, or them dying off, or having more deer brought in, or more being born. Everything has a balance. Even your body. Remember the proverb: All work and no play makes Jack a dull boy? It is all about balance. If you cannot find balance between what you enjoy doing and what you must do, you will find yourself spending too much time doing one thing and not the other, leading to you lacking something in your life. This is true even for your chakras. In the next section of this book we seek to show you how easy it can be to bring balance to your own life just by realigning your chakras.

Balancing Your Chakras

According to Schimdt (2019) and Mindvalley (2017), there are a wide range of things you can do to bring balance to your chakras. Each is unique and there is more than one method that you can use to try and find the perfect balance that you need in your life. Experiment and have fun.

Root Chakra

Your Root chakra is your connection to the physical realm, so think of yourself as a tree. What would a tree need to be happy? Water, sunshine, and the earth. Consider taking a leisurely stroll through a nature reserve or park (White, 2019). If you want something a little more strenuous maybe try a hike. Don't feel like exercise? How about a long relaxing shower or bath to help calm down those nerves that have been firing all day? We, however, are not trees, so instead of roots we have our legs. Take the time to do some leg strengthening and stretching exercises or some yoga to help move that energy from your Root chakra towards the earth. You can even dance a few quick steps if you have a sudden burst of energy, it doesn't matter if you are good at this or not. Feeling a little hungry after all that exercise? Don't forget that your Root chakra is represented by red, so any fruits or vegetables (apples, cherries, radishes, etc.) with that color is great to help you balance this node. Talking of color coding, consider adding a few pieces of red clothing or accessories to give your chakra a boost. Are you the kind of person that loves having their feet played with? Why not treat them to a massage or a pedicure? They have been doing all the heavy lifting, you know.

If you have an underactive Root chakra it is suggested that you try to reconnect with the physical realm by connecting with nature. So, if you are not interested in exercise, why not take your favorite activity and do it in the garden? Even gardening helps to bring a little more energy to this chakra.

If you have an overactive Root chakra, other activities include giving some of that excess energy away in the form of a gift. Volunteering your time and energy, random acts of kindness, or showing compassion are some sure ways to calm that excessive energy.

Your Root chakra is your foundation node. Because of this, it is a good idea to start aligning this chakra before moving onto your other chakras.

Sacral Chakra

This chakra is associated with intimacy, so a lot of your potential fixes has a lot to do with expressing yourself and dealing with your emotions. If you are someone who loves journaling, then it is strongly suggested that you pick up your favorite pen or pencil and jot down some thoughts (positive or negative) to help you express yourself. If you are not a wordsmith, why not find a nice quiet place and take the time to consider your thoughts and emotions in silence (Regan, 2020) whilst sitting in a cross-legged position. Other activities you can try are dancing as well as swimming. Not up to any of that? Maybe invite a friend out for a heart to heart to express your emotions. Talking to a therapist can also help with any anxiety you may have. If you are someone who enjoys the slower aspects of life, try a few stretches or yoga positions which concentrate on opening your hips. Remember that this chakra is associated with the color orange. Why not surround yourself with this stunning color? If you're journaling, maybe get yourself an orange journal, an orange pen, and maybe have an orange cup with your favorite beverage. Throw on that orange scarf to add a splash of color to appease this chakra.

An underactive Sacral chakra can be boosted by healthy snacking. Try to eat orange food that can be found in nature (oranges, sweet potatoes, etc.) and avoid artificial foods. Try to be creative even if you don't want to. Writing and painting is a great way to get those creative juices flowing. If you have found yourself becoming a bit of a recluse, why not reach out to a friend or allow yourself to find some intimacy?

To calm an overactive Sacral chakra, try to move some of that extra energy towards the Heart chakra. As you have to be wary of overindulgence why not practice restraint by asking yourself a few simple questions: Is this healthy? Can it benefit me or someone else? Do I NEED or WANT to eat the entire chocolate cake?

Solar Plexus Chakra

With this chakra, you need to form a relationship with yourself. People often say that you are your own worst enemy and that is somewhat true. No one is better at self-sabotage as the person doing it to themselves. This can be difficult, but Matluck (2019a) suggests that you make peace with your inner critic. The first thing you need to do is identify what you judge about yourself and then ask yourself if it is really necessary. Consider mirror-gazing exercises. Face yourself, face down those judgmental thoughts in your head and work on your affirmations. A good example that you can use is: I am enough. Thinking it is not enough. You need to say it and not in a little mouse voice. You need to convince yourself of what you are saying.

This can take some time, so don't be hard on yourself. Remember, you are trying to make friends with an enemy and that is not something that happens overnight. Every time you see yourself in a mirror, reaffirm your own affirmation.

This chakra is associated with the element of fire and the color yellow. Think fire and sunlight. Do you enjoy camping? If so, why not be the one to volunteer to make s'mores or do the cooking over the open fire? If you are not the outdoorsy type, try some sunbathing. When you take the time to enjoy the sun, vitamin D (thus known as the sunshine vitamin) is produced in your body and is vital to your health (Raman, 2018). Vitamin D has benefits such as telling your guts to absorb essential minerals like calcium and phosphorus, which aid in maintaining strong bones. Lack of vitamin D can have serious repercussions such as osteoporosis (weakened bones), depression, and in extreme cases, death. However, remember to go out into the sun sparingly or with the correct sunscreen products.

The position of this chakra is in the core of your body so if you like to exercise, target that area. With the color yellow, you are spoiled with many choices when it comes to food or drink. Whilst you are sunbathing, why not enjoy a lovely cool lemonade? If you are not a fan of something sweet, try lemon water for that refreshing boost to your body.

To treat an underactive Solar Plexus chakra, work on those affirmations by list building. Take all your good qualities and reaffirm that you are good at them. Combine this with your mirror-gazing exercises to build that friendship with your inner critic.

To soothe an overactive Solar Plexus chakra, try to picture yourself as a beacon of love. One that shines so brightly that it needs to share its light and warmth with others.

Heart Chakra

The movies had something right about the heart. It is our place of love, not just what we feel, but also what we can offer. The Heart chakra can be balanced by quite a few things. Firstly, go outside and take a deep breath and enjoy the fresh air. Don't slouch whilst doing this. Stand tall, open your chest to receive two full lungs full of fresh air. Feel your heart beating strongly as you momentarily hold your breath? Good! You have a great start. Start stretching those shoulders, upper back and move down into your arms and fingers. A great way to balance out the Heart chakra is self-care, self-love, and expressing your love for others. Challenge yourself by showing appreciation for people you don't like (Matluck, 2019b). Even volunteering unconditionally is guaranteed to give you that warm, fuzzy feeling in your chest.

Pink. Need more be said? The color pink or this chakra's associated color, green, is a sure way to make you look good and help with the Heart chakra's imbalance. This doesn't have to just be clothes! Found a cute pink eye shadow or blush you have been dying to try? Give it a whirl and see the difference!

An underactive Heart chakra is corrected by breaking down those walls you have built around your heart. Getting hurt is a natural part of our development, it is how you handle it that will bring you peace. Appreciate those that give you love and return it in kind. Giving the gift of love is as good as receiving it.

An overactive Heart chakra needs to be calmed. It is as easy as taking a soothing bath. Why not add some pink bubble bath solution to the water so you can truly relax? Remember, it is important for you to be kind to yourself. Think of all the things you love about yourself.

Throat Chakra

Our voice is important and no one wants to feel that they are not heard. To balance the Throat chakra, try singing your heart out. It doesn't matter what others think of you, as long as you are enjoying the power of your voice. Remember where this chakra is? Place your hand over it while you sing, you will feel the vibrations under your fingers. Not much of a singer or too shy? Try soothing drinks like warm teas (whichever is your favorite) or cool lemon water, which you can prepare freshly for when you need it. The Throat chakra doesn't need you to be the one to sing either, you can also sit quietly and listen to music that soothes you. Turquoise is the color you want when you need something to go with your Throat chakra. Consider something that you can wear close to your throat, such as a necklace or if you do not like that suggestion, look at wearing something that can go on your lapel.

Matluck (2019c) states that your word choice is something that plays a vital role in balancing your Throat chakra. Words have always held power and the way we use them can greatly influence us and those around us. Imagine that you just went to an interview for your dream job and all you can think about is: I hope I get this job. I need this job. I don't know what I will do if I don't get this job. You need to shift the power of your words from uncertainty to certainty: That job is mine. I got this! This is called positive manifestation and it will change your life!

An underactive Throat chakra requires you to speak. It doesn't matter about what or if people are around to hear you. If a tree falls in the forest does it make a sound? The answer is yes. Use your words to speak your truths, no one has to hear them for you to make use of your Throat chakra.

An overactive Throat chakra is a very dangerous chakra. Sticks and stones may break your bones but words will never harm you is horribly untrue. Words hurt and they leave wounds that can't be seen that will fester when unnoticed. Think carefully before saying something filled with a negative emotion like hate or anger. It takes one second to change "I hate you," to "I am angry, give me time to calm down."

Third Eye Chakra

The Third Eye chakra is all about visualizing. Pay attention to the messages that your body is trying to send you, it is doing this for a reason. Yoga with closed eyes is a great way to visualize the way you should be doing the various poses, which will be discussed at a later stage of this book. If you are nervous or concerned about balance, practice them with your eyes open first until you build up your confidence. Another way to balance this chakra is the art of journaling. There are two types of journaling you can try according to Matluck (2019d). The first is to document your wishes for certain parts of your life. There should be different wishes for different periods. Another type of journaling is writing down what you dream of at night. This one can be a little tricky, as quite a few people are unable to remember their dreams upon waking. There are a few ways to overcome this. The most popular is to keep a diary close on hand so when you wake, you can jot down what you can remember. However, this may be a bit difficult if you have a busy morning. If you are someone who has a more relaxed afternoon when compared to your morning, why not to meditate on what you dreamed about the night before? Once you have a clear idea of what you dreamed, put it to paper.

Feeling a little claustrophobic with your emotions and have no one to vent to? Act them out. If you are angry, punch your pillow. If you are happy, then laugh until you no longer can. The color blue is another great way to balance your Third Eye chakra. Consider your dream journals having blue covers or even writing in blue.

An underactive Third Eye chakra means you are too grounded in the physical realm. Consider spending time with yourself in silent contemplation. Listen to that inner voice and pay attention, it is trying to tell you something. Give yourself some time to meditate.

An overactive Third Eye chakra means you are too connected to the immaterial realm. Bring yourself back to earth by doing activities that allow you to come into contact with dirt, gardening for example, or taking a barefoot walk in a park. A little dirt never hurt anyone.

Crown Chakra

When trying to balance your final chakra, it is important for you to take note of any and all cycles around you (moon, night and day, menstrual, etc.) and how this affects your body (Matluck, 2019e). You will be surprised to see how often you are influenced by what happens naturally in the world around you. Having a bad day? Try making a gratitude diary where you journal all the things that you are grateful for and enjoy having in your life. If you like yoga, try a few inverted poses (if you are flexible), or if you are very brave you can try to do a headstand. Be careful as not to injure yourself.

Ask yourself: How can I be of service? We are individual people, yes, but we all make up the vast universe, so find out where you fit in and how you can make a difference to the rest of those that inhabit this realm with you. Think of the bigger picture. If you need to be reminded of that, why not take the time to stare at the ocean, the night's sky, or even at a forest? These places often remind people of how small they really are when compared to the universe. Lastly, try to share yourself with others. Take the time to volunteer and help those that are in need of help.

To boost an underactive Crown chakra, just remind yourself that you are human and that is okay. This experience is precious and you should get to enjoy it, but don't forget to add activities that help you join your consciousness with the immaterial realm. Meditation is one of the easiest ways to do this.

Maintaining Healthy Chakras

We all know how difficult it can be to maintain a healthy diet and exercise, and there is no real difference when it comes to our chakras. A healthy chakra can easily be disrupted by anything, however, there are a lot of ways to keep your chakras healthy. For example, if you are drawn to a specific color when getting dressed (Destination Delux, n.d.), listen to that inner voice. Craving certain foods—eat (in moderation); drawn to certain sounds, music, or songs —listen. Feeling panicky but your inner voice is telling you to remain calm, try your affirmations to calm yourself. Other calming things you can try is to burn some incense or use essential oils, taking note of which scents best work for you. Try to be creative with your journaling (different colored pens, pasting in pictures, etc.), singing or even taking the time to smell the flowers on your way to work. A whole book could be written about this alone. The best advice that can be given is that you need to find what brings you peace and strive to do that. Be wary of overdoing anything that can cause your chakras to become unbalanced. Remember, everything in moderation is good for you.

Chapter 4:
Chakras, Meditation, and Yoga

The beginning of this book was to teach you about what the different chakras are, how they can be out of balance, and how to create balance in them. The next few chapters will introduce various other holistic or therapeutic means that can assist you in creating more positive energy to help maintain those chakras you have worked so hard on. This chapter specifically deals with meditation and yoga. If this is something you are not interested in or have mastered already, skip on ahead to the other chapters.

Brief History of Meditation

The understanding and practice of meditation may well be older than that of the understanding of chakras (Everly & Lating, 2002) with wall art found in India around about 5000-3500 BCE showing the typical meditation pose before it was written about in the Vedas, which was about 1500 BCE (Giovanni, 2018). It is assumed that knowledge of meditation was handed down orally before it was even penned down onto paper. The practice of mediation was not limited to India, but rather spread throughout the world as time progressed. Other Eastern countries which picked up the practice were first China and later towards the middle ages, Japan (Dumoulin et al., 2005a; 2005b). Towards the West, it was Philo of Alexandria in 20 BCE that wrote about meditation as spiritual exercises, which needed attention and concentration from the person attempting it. He wasn't the only one. Close to the third century, Plotinus came up with his own meditative practices (Urs, 1989), which sadly did not impress the Christians of the age even though Saint Augustine tried them but failed to achieve what he wanted from them. Other forms of meditation can be found in Kabbalistic practices (Brill, 2005) and even Islamic mysticism (Zaleski & Zaleski, 2005). Further spread of this practice westwards was almost complete in the late 19th century due to travel from other parts of the world. However, it wasn't until 1893, when the World Parliament of Religions was held in Chicago that most westerners started to take notice of the concept of meditation (Murphy et al., 1999).

So the concept of meditation is steeped in history, but what does it actually mean? How can we define meditation? This is something that is quite hotly debated amongst those that practice it. It can mean inner peace to one while it can mean enlightenment to another. In short: Meditation is what it needs to be to the person who needs it at that moment.

Meditations to Aid Your Chakras

Meditation requires you to find a quiet place where you can comfortably sit and not be disturbed for the duration of time you set out for yourself. There is an old Zen saying: "You should sit in meditation for 20 minutes a day, unless you're too busy; then you should sit for an hour." Basically, this is telling you that the busier you are, the more you are in need of a good meditation session. Consider that for a few minutes before just thinking you need a quick meditation session on a busy day.

The very first thing you need to do is sit in the typical meditative state, however, keep your hands with palms up on your knees (Mindvalley, 2019). Remember how you visualized your chakras earlier? Use the colors given to the chakras to help you meditate on each of the nodes. Energy must move, if a node is unmoving, you need to get it moving. Think as to why it may not be moving. Has something happened in your life recently? Have you forgotten something important that you should be doing to keep your internal energies happy? It is important that you start from the Root chakra and move up towards the crown. Don't skip any of the nodes. They are all important. Once you are able to meditate freely on your Crown chakra then there is a positive flow of energy that is unhindered throughout your whole body.

If you are finding meditation too difficult, don't give up! You need to dedicate time and energy to experience this to its full potential. It is important to remember that meditation is not about clearing your mind. You cannot switch your brain off! It is designed to think. Meditation is about repurposing your thoughts into something that is more constructive to what you need. Not everyone is able to change their thoughts from potential to certainty, so if you still find that you are unable to reach a good position in your meditation why not try some guided meditation sessions? Many online platforms or apps offer assistance in this regard. The important thing to remember is that you must find what works for you.

There are many types of chakra balancing meditations and each is different in its functions. The most common are the balancing and healing meditations that can be done (Digital Welt, n.d.). The aim of the balancing meditation is to create harmony in your body by releasing toxic energies that are trapped. These meditations are for opening and clearing chakras. The healing meditation is a two-part process.

The first part concentrates on the cause of your discomfort or negative feelings. What caused you to feel the way you do? Is it a physical problem? Mental? Emotional? Only once you are able to answer that question will you be able to move onto the second part. Here, you need to work on easing the effects of the way you feel. It doesn't help to just be aware of how you feel. You need to work through it and come out on the other end feeling like the problem has been resolved within you.

Mantras

If it is the focus you are missing in your meditation, why not try some vocalization in forms of mantras? The mind likes to wander and wonder, which can be a problem when you want to focus on a specific chakra. These mantras are aimed at each chakra and allow you to solely concentrate on a specific node of energy. You can either use Sanskrit (Yugay, 2019) or English (Gregory, 2018) to help you with your focus.

To specifically focus on your Root chakra, chant LAM or *I am*. For the Sacral chakra, use VAM or *I feel*. The Solar Plexus chakra's vocalization is RAM or *I do*. YAM is used for the Heart chakra, but you can also say *I love*. The Throat chakra focus mantra is HAM or *I speak*. The Third Eye chakra is UAM / OM or *I see*. Lastly, to meditate on the Crown chakra, you may do so in silence if you wish or use the vocalization OM / AH (to symbolize release of energy). The English version of this is *I understand,* because once you reach this stage of your meditation you will understand the universe in part.

However, if you are not sure which chakra is the problem, try some non-specific mantras to help you with the focus you need. The mantra of OM is used to move energy from the lower plane to the higher plane, and this is why it is usually used for the Third Eye and Crown chakras. KRIM (pronounced k-reem) is a mantra which helps with energizing the lower chakras to cleanse the body. SHRIM (sh-reem) is the mantra which aids the Third Eye and Crown chakra and gifts body and spiritual health. HRIM (h-reem) is the mantra of healing creativity. This mantra boosts your passion and purifies your heart. HUM (hoom) mantra is meant to destroy negativity and aids in spreading positivity and vitality through your whole body.

Mantras are highly specific but nothing stops you on expanding them to help you with your own personal chakra cleansing. If you have experienced a terrible heartbreak lately, why not consider something along the lines of: *I'm still capable of love. I represent love.* See what makes you comfortable but remember, you cannot lie to yourself. Only speak truths to aid your meditation and clear chakras.

A Brief History of Yoga

The way we understand yoga today is not at all like it was in the past. Yoga Sutras of Patanjali gained great success in the west during the late 19th century after it was introduced by Swami Vivekananda (White, 2014). Outside of India, yoga developed into the relaxation and stress relief technique that concentrated on specific poses often seen as a form of exercise many people enjoy today (Burley, 2000). However, this is not its whole meaning. Upon returning to India, you would find that the practice of yoga is more than just mere exercise. It also has a meditative and spiritual component to it (Burley, 2000 & Cobb & Rumbold, 2012).

Let's delve into the history of what yoga is. The word yoga comes from the Sanskrit *Yuj* meaning to attach or to join (Saraswati, 2008). The spiritual aspect of this word is noted in Yoga Sutras of Patanjali, where the aim of this practice was the unity between the human spirit and that of the Divine (Monier et al., 2005). No one can agree upon the date when yoga started but people can agree on where it began: Ancient India (~3000-1500 BCE) (Crangle, 1994). From here, it was developed by many people during many eras. Notably, this includes the practice of Buddhism, the teachings of Patanjali, Hatha Yoga, and Modern Postural Yoga.

Lee et al. (2015) wrote in depth about the above-mentioned practices. Let's start with Siddhartha Gautama, or better known by his more famous name: Buddha. His yoga teachings were meant to bring mindfulness to what we do in our everyday situations. He did this in two ways. The first was his core understanding called "The Four Noble Truths" and the second was the practice of these truths called "The Noble Eightfold Path."

The four Truths are described as the following: The truth of suffering (this is inevitable), the truth of the cause of the suffering (things in our life are the causes of our misery), the truth of the end of suffering (all suffering comes to an end), and finally, the truth of the path that leads to the end of suffering (what is required of us to end the suffering). What does this all mean? Buddha is basically telling us that life is suffering, you cannot avoid it and must simply live with it as best you can, as it is not eternal. All things pass, good and bad.

The fourth Truth leads into the Noble Eightfold Path. What do we have to do to end things that cause us to suffer? The first is the Wise (or Right) View; this is the path of understanding what is right and wrong, and knowing that there are consequences to all our actions. The second is Wise Intention; this is the path of kindness and not having the intent to cause harm to anything. The third path is Wise Speech, basically, watch what you say, no lies, no gossip, and no abuse. The fourth path is Wise Action; beware of your actions—murder, theft, or sexual misconduct are things that should be avoided at all costs. The fifth path is Wise Livelihood; earn your livelihood from activities that do not harm others. The sixth path is Wise effort; striving to achieve states of mind and body that are good for you. The seventh path is Wise Mindfulness; be wary of your actions and don't be absent minded about it. The eighth path is Wise Concentration; this is the unity of all mindfulness through meditation.

Generally, it is found that those of the west prefer to migrate towards this practice if they wish to work on their mind, whilst those that purely wish to work on their bodies move onto more physical aspects of yoga.

The more physical part of yoga is later seen in Patanjali's Yoga Sutra with *The Eight Limbs of Yoga*. Yama is the practice of restraint and upholding your morals (Newlyn, n.d.). Niyama is all about looking after yourself. Asana concentrates on posture, normally of your meditative position. Pranayama concentrates on breathing techniques and how it can affect our mind. Pratyahara is often misunderstood, as it is known as sense withdrawal. This does not mean we lose our sense, but rather that they are not a distraction when we meditate. Dharana is about focusing your concentration to allow meditation. Dhyana, in which during this stage you are truly meditating with no distraction. Lastly, you have Samadhi, which is where you achieve enlightenment, yet this is still more meditative than a physical representation of yoga.

The first practice to bring action to its teachings was Hatha Yoga, which concentrated on practices for breathing and postures, sexual energy control, and meditation. This is where we start to see where our modern yoga comes from. It was during the 20th century when two lines of teaching allowed for Modern Postural Yoga (MPY) to be born. We have Swami Sivananda of Rishikesh and Krishnamacharya of Mysore to thank for this achievement.

Yoga has come a far way from its pure meditative form to the postural practices seen today. It has been influenced by time, people, and different practices, and will likely in the future continue to evolve into something that will bring peace of mind and body to whoever needs it.

Yoga Poses to Aid Chakras

To list all the possible yoga poses from the different disciplines would probably require a whole new book to describe them all. Those listed below are yoga poses that are aimed to clear your seven main chakras (Editors, 2014; Moules, n.d.; Mourya, 2019), but do not let that limit you on what you are capable of doing. A comprehensive list and images of yoga can be found from many sources. Remember, take care in performing any kind of exercise, no matter how easy it appears.

Root Chakra

Try the Mountain Pose. Stand up straight with your feet planted firmly on the ground. Bring your palms together in front of your chest whilst relaxing your shoulders. Visualize the red chakra reaching to the ground as well as upwards. Take a few deep breaths before releasing this pose. Other poses that are good for this chakra include the Tree Pose (Fig. 2) and Child's Pose.

Fig. 2. Tree Pose.

Sacral Chakra

Try the revolved Triangle Pose. Start by standing up straight with your arms over your head. Step forward with your right leg and bring your left towards the inside of your right foot. Here it would be a good idea to have a yoga block to rest your hand on. Twist your hips to the right as your right hand extends to the sky. Follow that hand with your gaze. Hold for a few breaths then switch to the left side. More poses that are good for this chakra include the Goddess Pose, Yoga Squat, Butterfly Pose, and Extended Side Angle Pose.

Solar Plexus Chakra

Try the Boat Pose. Sit upon the ground with your knees bent before you. Lift your arms towards your toes and open your chest by leaning backwards. If you want more of a challenge, raise your feet and be prepared to activate your core. Hold this pose for about 15-30 seconds before relaxing and trying it a few more times. A few more good poses include the Reverse Plant, Bow Pose, and Crescent Pose (Fig. 3).

Fig. 3. Crescent pose.

Heart Chakra

For this chakra why not try the Low Lunge? Stand in a typical lunge position with your right leg extended forward. Lower your left knee to the ground while your left hand rests on the back of it. Raise your right hand above your head and lift your face skywards. Take a deep breath, hold, then release. You can repeat this with your left leg leading instead of right. Other poses that are great for this chakra include the Camel Pose, Upward Facing Dog, Fish Pose, and Tree Pose.

Fig 4. Upward Facing Dog.

Throat Chakra

For the Throat chakra you can simply sit in the Easy Pose (Fig. 5). Sit in your typical meditative pose and allow your chin to come close to your throat. Inhale deeply and relax those shoulders. Concentrate on your hand positions. The thumb and index finger should be touching with the back of your hands resting on your knees. If you are not shy, try chanting the mantra *Humee Hum Brahm Hum.* If you are shy, hum it or even sing your favorite song. This pose can be kept for 3-11 minutes. If you want something a little more athletic, why not try the Wheel Pose, Supported Shoulder Stand, or Cat Cow Pose.

Fig. 5. Easy Pose.

Third Eye Chakra

The Dolphin Pose can be a bit channeling, so be wary of your shoulder strength. From a standing position, bring your hands down to touch the ground, keeping your legs as straight as possible (Downward Facing Dog Pose). Lower yourself to your forearms and bring your hands together with thumbs pointing up and pinkies on the ground. This is your Dolphin Pose. Now slowly rock forward to bring your chin to your thumbs then return to the Dolphin Pose. Repeat this up to ten times. Other poses you can try include a Handstand, Forward Folds, and Pigeon Pose (Fig. 6).

Fig. 6. Pigeon pose.

Crown Chakra

Here is another challenging pose for you to try: The Butterfly Pose. From a standing position, sink into a squat on the balls of your feet, then open your knees until your heels touch. Bring your hands together before your heart. If you want even more of a challenge, raise your hands above your head. Hold this pose for 5-10 breaths, then release. Now, if you want something a lot easier, try the Corpse Pose, Saddle Pose, or the Lotus Pose (Fig. 7).

Fig. 7. Lotus Pose.

Not comfortable with yoga or meditation? These are not your only choices to realign your chakras. There are many other means for you to ascertain balance. It is important for you to find what you are comfortable with. If you are not comfortable, your body will know and you will not get the balance that you are seeking.

There are still a few chapters left. Continue reading to see what can bring you balance.

Chapter 5:
Chakras and Crystals

The Earth is bountiful not only in the beauty that it shows us but also in what it gifts to us. It provides nutrition to us through the food it produces. It provides us shelter in forms of stone and earth, some of which is still used in its raw form in various places of the world. The Earth also provides what we humans term as precious materials such as metals (gold, copper, etc.) and precious stones (diamonds, rubies, etc.). Now we all know that not everyone is able to afford these precious materials but our planet knows this and provides us with what we call semi-precious stones (our definitions, not the Earth's), which many people have been exposed to in one form or another.

Fig. 8. Colorful gemstones.

History of Crystal Healing

Before we can start with the history of crystal healing, we need to start with our relationship with crystals. This relationship dates back thousands of years. The word crystal itself comes from the Greek word *krystallos* (Shashkevich, 2018) which roughly means "coldness drawn together," as they thought that it was a form of ice that never melted. The next time you hold a crystal in your hand, you will feel for yourself that the name holds true. Amongst the people of the west, crystal is often seen as decorations for objects of power (i.e. religious artifacts) and was often used to describe the purity of something. Think crystal clear waters as a good example of this. However, these crystals also hold a mysterious side to them. Those of color, for example, amethyst, appear to be dark at first, but if you take the time to truly look at them you will find that many of them are more transparent. During the middle ages, people believed that these stones held some kind of spiritual aspect about them. People wished to be able to hold something physical which represented their faith in something bigger than themselves. This craving still exists today.

As people, we also like to assign value to many kinds of crystals. Think of the value of a diamond when compared to that of a rose quartz. It is somewhat vastly different. We don't only assign value to crystals, but we also assign special meaning to them. You may have heard of birthstones before or maybe you are even aware of what your own birthstone is. Brightly colored gemstones are assigned to different months of the year and each has its own meaning. Birthstones make great gifts and can be bought as loose gemstones or as simple or unique jewelry pieces fit for both men or women.

The concept of using crystals to heal is not a new one. Lapidary medicine (the use of crystals to heal most ailments) was something that was believed by many people of many different cultures throughout the world (Moore & McClean, 2010). This knowledge was collected into books called Lapidaries. During modern times, crystal healing is strongly associated with the New Age Spiritual movement (Regal, 2009).

Practitioners who use crystals in their healing ceremonies use those of a certain color or those that show certain metaphysical qualities. These crystals will be placed on different parts of the body, depending on what is needed by the person who has come to see the practitioner.

Crystal healing is an alternative healing technique and is considered a pseudoscience, as there is no way for science to prove whether they actually work as what the practitioners of this technique claims it to. However, Palermo (2017) argued for the cause of crystal healing by saying that scientists and doctors naturally couldn't prove that crystals have any effect on diseases, as the diseases have never been proved to have an effect on the inner energies of the body. Regardless of there being no scientific proof that crystal healing actually works, it remains popular amongst many people. Why?

To put it simply, a person is able to relax when they go through the therapeutic practice. Most problems in today's society are that we are rushing everywhere and causing unnecessary stress to ourselves. Taking a moment to slow down and destress could be all we need to start to feel normal again.

Crystal healing goes quite well with trying to bring balance to chakras as the practice also makes use of color and specific positions for healing sites. In fact, there are very specific stones for each chakra as well as different ailments to the body.

Which Crystals Help Which Chakra?

Like meditation and yoga, you need to give yourself some time to be able to go through all the steps of crystal healing. This needs to be done in a place of quiet where you will not be disturbed by anything (this includes your phone) for about 30 minutes. Your next step is to be very clear in your intentions for this healing process. What do you want from this? Then, you need to ensure your crystals are cleaned. No, I don't mean polished, I mean take the time to take care of the crystals' energies by cleaning them with cool water or alternatively, leave them in a place where they can receive direct sunlight or moonlight (Chakra Healing, 2014 & Lizzy, 2019). The shapes of your stones are completely up to you but remember, sharp points accompanying a heavy stone could end in injury. Rather, stick to something that is easily handled; small smooth stones are suggested. Last, but not least, it is important to be grateful towards the stones. Remember, they are a gift from the Earth and if you handle them with negative emotions, they are affected by them. Bless each stone you use in your healing with positive energy and thoughts before you begin. It is important to note the following: For this healing to be efficient, you as the user needs to believe that the stones can help you with your healing process (Lizzy, 2019). A little meditation on your intentions with the stones also helps to move negative energies from your body.

So now you know how to clear the energies of your stones, but how do you choose the right stone for the job? First of all, be conscious of your intentions and your body. What has been out of sorts the last few days? Have you had any illnesses that are centered to a certain part of your body? Once you are able to answer those questions, look over your collection of stones. Are you attracted to any of them as you run your hands over them? Do some of them stand out more than others? Listen to your intuition and choose those stones to work with. Don't limit yourself on just having the stones within your house. If a certain stone stands out more than others on a daily basis, why not consider carrying it around with you? Chakra stone jewelry is quite popular in forms of necklaces or bracelets.

We have selected our crystals but what do we do now? Step One: Select the places you want to concentrate on. Step two: Place the crystals you want to use. Step three: Concentrate on your intentions by visualizing a white, clearing energy entering your body with each breath you take in. Step four: Exhale, allowing the negative energies and stresses to leave your body. Thoughts have more power than what you believe, so keep your thoughts on imagining this process clearly. Step five: As you allow this clearing energy into your body, direct it to the places where you need energy activated (for underactive chakras) or calmed (overactive chakras). There may be some resistance in some of your chakras, so take your time clearing them. Remember, each chakra is part of a whole, if you skip over a particularly difficult one it will remain unbalanced and will pull your freshly balanced chakras out of alignment should you ignore it for too long.

As mentioned before, this is a timely process. Leave the stones in the positions where you had them for between 10-15 minutes (depending on the time you need). If they fall off, don't worry, you can simply replace them. If they continue to fall off, leave them, it will not influence the healing if they are a little ways off from their intended position. As this is a timely process, you need to guard your thoughts from negative aspects. Concentrate on the positive or the problems will persist.

Finally, once you feel that your chakras have received what they needed, you will have to clean your crystals once more. Don't forget to thank them for the assistance they have granted you.

Another important thing to remember is that chakras are color dependent. If you are attracted to a certain stone, but it is not on the list below and it matches the chakra color then trust your instincts. Your body knows what it needs. You may do the healing sitting or lying down, whichever brings you more comfort is the one you should choose. So, just in case you have forgotten about the position of the chakra or its associated color, it will be repeated for your convenience instead of you having to page back and forth, as that is no fun in a book!

Root Chakra

The Root chakra is located at the base of your spine and it associates with the color red. If you wish to concentrate on this particular chakra, first determine whether you have an underactive or overactive node. For an underactive node try giving it energy by using crystals like bloodstone, ruby, or garnet. For an overactive node try grounding it by using crystals like black tourmaline, hematite, red or brown jasper, and onyx.

Sacral Chakra

The Sacral chakra is found slightly under your belly button and is usually associated with the color orange. For an underactive Sacral chakra look at using carnelian, sunstone, or even golden topaz to give it the energy it deserves. To ground an overactive chakra consider using red jasper or peach calcite. Other good crystals include moonstones and coral.

Solar Plexus Chakra

The location of this chakra can be found just under your last set of ribs and is associated with the color yellow. For an underactive chakra make use of golden topaz or malachite. To help ground the overactive chakra use a tiger's eye or ametrine.

Heart Chakra

This chakra is found in the center of your breastbone close to the heart and is associated with the color green. To energize the underactive chakra, make use of a piece of rose quartz and to ground the overactive node, use a moss agate. Jade is also a great crystal to work with for both reasons.

Throat Chakra

The Throat chakra can be found at the base of your throat and is governed by the color blue. To help with a weak node use an aqua aura or blue topaz. To calm an overactive node, try some aquamarine or blue lace agate. This is a great chakra to keep balanced with a necklace you can wear every day.

Third Eye Chakra

The Third Eye chakra is found between your two physical eyes on your forehead and is represented by the color indigo. Underactive chakras can be boosted with sapphire, blue topaz, or even quartz. The overactive chakra can be soothed by the use of lapis lazuli or amethyst.

Crown Chakra

The Crown chakra is a little above your head, so just place the crystal on the top of your head if you are sitting or slightly away from your head if you are lying down. This chakra is associated with the color white or violet. The crystals that can be used for this chakra include selenite, celestite, and even a chrysanthemum stone.

Placing of Crystals

Sometimes we are not sure of what we want from these crystals, so don't just limit yourself to just balancing your chakras. Combine crystals and meditation to see what you need from your life. There are hundreds of different crystals and gemstones that can aid in many aspects of your life (Rekstis, 2019).

Meditate on what is wrong in your life and then find the correct crystal that can aid you in your problems.

If you are seeking protection from physical and emotional negativity in your life, consider keeping a piece of obsidian (a black crystal) close by. This stone is also said to help with various emotional blockages and can help with physical problems such as digestive issues.

Are you prone to sleepless nights? Consider keeping an amethyst (a purple crystal) close to your bed. This stone is said to help with sleeplessness and even offer protection, as well as having healing properties. Physically it is said to help with the alleviation of stress, which definitely would help for those sleepless nights.

Feeling that terrible writer's block or just cannot find the inspiration you desperately need to complete something? Keep a tiger's eye (a soft brown/red/green striped crystal) on hand, either as a loose gem or something that can be worn. This beautiful crystal aids in boosting your motivation whilst easing things like self-doubt and anxiety. If you need your mind clear to aid you in making good choices, this is the crystal for you.

Those are just a few problems that can be alleviated by some crystals. Do your own research to find the right crystal for you. On the other hand, if you want to go on your gut feeling, why not visit your local shop that sells crystals and gems. Here, you are able to spend hours looking for the right crystal in the crystal pits or you can buy something right off of the shelves. Listen to your intuition when searching.

Chakras are not the only places in your life that need clearing of negative energies. You cannot hope to keep your chakras clear if the areas you expose yourself to aren't treated in the same manner you treat yourself. Let's look at how crystals can be used in our own homes or place of work to cleanse and protect (Askinosie, 2019).

Let's start with our home away from home: the office space. We spend many hours in this location and it is important to cleanse it of negative thoughts and energies. Shungite is a great crystal if you are surrounded by electronics all day long. This crystal is known for the special property of absorbing and neutralizing electromagnetic radiation (EMF). If you are finding yourself lacking in energy, try bringing a pyrite crystal. This stone is said to promote creative thinking and business opportunities.

Many people tend to complain about sleeplessness or being unable to relax enough to fall asleep. An easy crystal to find and use in the bedroom is the rose quartz. This crystal is also great for your heart chakra and all the emotions associated with it. Naturally, just look at the beautiful pink coloration. This crystal can also help ease negative emotions like anger, which you should not go to bed with. The rose quartz isn't just good for partners but also for families, as the emotion of love is spread through this crystal. Alternatively, if you are looking for peaceful sleep, why not consider a selenite stone?

If you are a family unit with a few kids, consider using celestite crystals to create a calming and soothing environment in their rooms. Kiddies have great imaginations and they truly believe that scary tree outside of the window is a monster trying to get them. Blue lace agate helps to calm their anxieties, so place one on their bedside table before they go to sleep. Please be wary of the size of the crystal and the age of your child. We do not want a choking hazard in a place a young one can reach. Always place possible choking hazards far away from little hands.

Even keeping your kitchen clear of negativity is important. It is used to create our nourishment and if it is made in a negative environment, it will affect us. Carnelian is the perfect crystal when it comes to being creative whilst cooking. Cooking for a family can be a daunting task, so why not add a citrine to the windowsill to give you the positivity you need when cooking?

The living room is the space where the family can gather and enjoy time together. The amethyst is an ideal crystal if you want to create a positive space for your family. If you know someone is coming to visit who is known to stir up trouble, consider putting a fluorite in the center of the room (on a coffee table for example). This should help with the harmony, though we cannot guarantee this will work for all in-laws.

The bathroom is another place of sanctuary and the best crystal for this is Himalayan salt rock to aid in purifying this area. Add a few small rocks to dissolve in your bathwater so that you relax and enjoy as your tensions melt away. If you are not a fan of things in the water with you, or you prefer to shower, why not try clear quartz? This crystal is known for its purifying aspects. Place this on the edge of the bath or in the shower.

The front door is your first line of defense to your home, so it is a good idea to stop negative energies at the door. Try some black tourmaline to add some extra protection to your home. With this crystal stationed at the entrance of your home, it is able to purify anything that walks through the door, thus leaving the negativity at the doormat as it is not welcome.

If you are lucky enough to have a garden, you can create an area of protection there too! Even if you have a few potted plants, this is a sure way to ensure they survive your "green thumb." Get some green aventurine and bury it in the soil to help with growth in your plants. If you wish to create a space for silent contemplation, consider placing some quartz crystals all around the garden and power them with good intentions every time you water your garden.

Chapter 6:
Chakras and Essential Oils

Imagine for a moment that you are walking down a busy street. People are rushing all around you and you yourself are trying to get to work. Something wafts past your nose. It takes you a second to recognize the smell. Fresh bread. Memories come to mind. These are not memories of you enjoying that grilled cheese sandwich yesterday. No, these memories are from a time much further in your past. You, as a child, your feet barely touching the floor from the chair you are sitting on. You are eagerly swinging your feet in anticipation. The kitchen you are sitting in belongs to your late grandmother and she is busying herself with something in the oven. She has baked some fresh bread and you will be the one to have the first, fresh slice. You can almost taste the warm bread and the salty butter. The memory is so strong that you are compelled to stop at the bakery to get yourself something to quell the sudden hunger. Do you have a similar memory to this? Many people do. Why do smells trigger memories in us? That has to do with the structure of our brains (Beeler, 2014). The area which processes what we smell is very close to the part of the brain that handles our emotional memories. Smells are important to us, both pleasant or disgusting. We use deodorants to cover our smell or perfumes or cologne to enhance ourselves. What if I told you that smells can help you balance your chakras? With the use of essential oils, this is more than possible.

History of Essential Oils

According to history, the first type of essential oil was being used in Egypt, Persia, and India (Georg Urdang et al., 1948). The oil mentioned was called oil of turpentine, and appeared many times throughout history. Though it was mentioned how it was made, that was not something that was added to paper until Pliny (23-79 BCE), a Roman historian of natural history, noted the crude distillation process of his era. This process included parts of the plant of interest (flowers or roots; sometimes whole, other times crushed) added to the best rendered fat (best possible quality of the time) in a container, which was then left outside in the sun. After some time, the oil was released from the plant and mixed with the rendered animal fat. Crude but effective, as the scent sought after was obtained.

A similar process was noted by Joanne Mesue in his book *Grabaddin* in the middle of the thirteenth century. However, he noted more oils, such as oil of juniper and oil of asphaltum. Oils from plants were often seen as a byproduct of creating distilled waters and it was not always a welcomed one. It was Arnald de Villanova, a Catalan physician, who continued to improve on the distillation process of removing the essential oils. He was well known for the qualities of his distilled water (think rose water and not drinking water). At this stage the use of fire was used to help the distillation process and no longer just the sun.

The name 'essential' oils was coined by Paracelsus von Hohenheim. He used the phrase *Quinta essentia* (quintessence), which referred to the part of the drug (medicine) which was the most effective. He believed that the isolation of this compound should be the goal of the study of pharmacology.

In Brunschwig's book *Liber De Arte Distillandi,* he described the distillation techniques being used as well as added more oils that were previously not distilled. Included now was oil of rosemary and oil of spike (lavender). However, the cost of these substances were incredibly expensive and not at all popular. Walter Reiff, a physician, tried the current method of distillation and found that it only worked for some things and not all. He tried his luck at trying to get oil from saffron and did not get the results he got from lavender or rosemary. However, this distillation still didn't result in a pure oil.

During the sixteenth and eighteenth centuries it was mostly pharmacists who dabbled in the distillation of essential oils. As time moved on, essential oils were no longer being used in the medical field but rather found their way into the perfume trade, food, or drinks. Irrespective, it was O. Wallach, F.W. Semmler, their students, and collaborators that brought about the "Elizabethan Age" for the industry of essential oils. It was thanks to them that many more different oils were discovered and put into use.

This process even found its way to America during the later half of the eighteenth century, though the oil that was concentrated on was the oil of turpentine from the vast pine forests. It wasn't until the nineteenth century that a few indigenous species were used to produce oils; the American wormseed and wintergreen. It was later in this century that the more better-known oils (peppermint and a variety of citrus) were being produced.

Where does this leave the industry today? In a pretty good position actually. The current value of the essential oil market is $18.62 billion, as of May 2020 (Grand View Research, 2020) because of potential uses of the various oils.

The process of collecting the oils is much more refined now, with it being collected either through steam distillation or cold press from the desired plant (West, 2019). We still use these oils for perfume, creams, and cooking essences (think vanilla or peppermint essence). These oils are also used in Aromatherapy, which is a kind of alternative medicine that is used to aid relaxation (Lee et al., 2012).

If you are thinking of using essential oils or you have some essential oils it is key to know how to use them correctly. Essential oils in their pure distilled form are dangerous and act as poison if swallowed (Lee et al., 2019). We all remember the trick our parents pulled on us when we had our first smell of vanilla essence. It smells great but tastes horrific. If you have young children, please ensure that your essential oils are well out of reach or you may have to call your local Poison Center for instructions on how to handle accidental swallowing of these substances.

Another warning is to not place the essential oil directly on your skin as this can cause anything from a skin irritation to an allergic reaction (Bleasel et al., 2002). Because of the problem with contact dermatitis, essential oils need to be in another substrate before being added to the skin. This substrate is called a carrier oil and some popular ones being used in the industry include avocado oil, coconut oil, or even vegetable oil.

If you are not sure if you may or may not be allergic, do a standard reaction test; the same test you do when you try a new cream or deodorant. Unsure of how to do this? Take a small amount of what you want to test (essential oil mixed in its carrier oil) and rub it into a small area of your forearm. If it itches or burns, wash the area immediately and cease using the product. If nothing happens, keep an eye on it for about an hour. If there is no reaction during this time you should be fine. If you are still unsure, speak to your doctor about a scratch test. This test involves making tiny scratches on your back or arm to see if you are allergic to up to 50 different types of allergens (dust, cat hair, etc).

Scents and Essential Oils to Match Your Chakras

As each chakra has its own unique position and characteristics, the essential oils that are used for each one is also unique. There are a few ways you can use the oils in helping you realign your chakras. One is to directly apply the essential oil in its carrier oil to the chakra's bodily location that you wish to concentrate on or consider a diffuser or nebulizer to release the scent into the air (Aura Cacia, n.d.; Grande, 2018). Please read all warnings before deciding which method you wish to try. If you do not like the scents suggested, know that there are many possible scents and oils you can choose from. Choose what you believe will work for you. You can also choose to apply the oils yourself or have it done with a massage by an aromatherapist.

If you prefer something a little less touchy, there are other methods of using essential oils in your life (Perfect Potion, n.d.). Are you someone who enjoys long, relaxing baths? A teaspoon of your chosen oil dissolved into your bathwater is exactly what is needed. Once the oil is dissolved into the water and not an oily film floating around, you can submerge yourself in the water for between 15-20 minutes (more if you like to top up with hot water after some time). Are you leading a life which is too busy? Why not consider dabbing a small droplet of your chosen oil to a handkerchief or tissue and carry it around with you? Smell it when you find yourself in need of a reminder of what you are trying to achieve in your life.

If you are lucky enough to have a space of your own that you have set up for meditation and you have some crystals you use, why not consider using your chosen essential oil on them? A small drop on your crystals or gemstones is all they need to enhance their power to help you achieve what you want.

Root Chakra

For this chakra, why not use some patchouli essential oil? This oil is perfect for someone who is comfortable with being able to stand on their own two feet. It can also help with feelings of fatigue and negative emotions. Don't like the smell? Not a fan? No worries! Like crystals, there is more than one scent that can go with this chakra. Try cypress oil to give you the soothing you need.

If you are comfortable with a foot massage this is a great way to interact with your chakra. For an underactive chakra, try some nutmeg whilst an overactive chakra does well with vetiver. If you want to maintain a chakra that is already balanced, use bergamot orange oil.

Sacral Chakra

Neroli essential oil is great for this chakra. It helps give you the energy to love (yourself and others), banish any of your sorrows, and bring peace. If you need a bit of boost to your ability to find hope, this is a great oil for you. Other oils you can use include patchouli and ylang-ylang.

A great place to get massaged for this chakra is your lower back. If this node is a little sleepy, wake it up with some cardamom oil whilst the previous mentioned oils are great for soothing an overactive node. To maintain a healthy chakra, try using some sandalwood or sweet orange.

Solar Plexus Chakra

To clear the air of all negativity try some pine essential oil. This oil is great to help you move forward after emotional problems that have caused you to become jaded. Another great oil you can consider is ginger, if you do not mind it triggering memories of baking ginger cookies.

Dogs were right about one thing: Tummy rubs are the best! A soothing tummy rub is the way to go if you want this chakra massaged. If you have a chakra that is a little sluggish, make use of eucalyptus or juniper berry oil. An overactive chakra is better handled by applying some vetiver or helichrysum. If you find yourself with a well-balanced Solar Plexus chakra, then keep it that way with some lemon or grapefruit oil.

Heart Chakra

Ironically enough, rosewood or rose essential oil is great for your Heart chakra. This aids with the flow of emotions and helps you to make peace with any feelings you may be experiencing. If you are holding onto any negative or repressed feelings, this oil will help you release your hold on them. Other possible oils you could use include pine and neroli.

Depending on your comfort levels with someone else massaging you, you can either be massaged along the breastbone or the middle of your back. To help you open that Heart chakra make use of palmarosa, whilst if you want something a little more calming, try lavender or marjoram. A balanced Solar Plexus chakra is maintained as such with the use of geranium essential oil.

Throat Chakra

A great oil for this chakra is lavender oil. The Throat chakra is your voice and this oil encourages you to share your gifts with the world. Shy? That's alright, it can also help you to communicate efficiently and bring meaning to your words.

Not many people like to have their necks touched, so why not try a body spray with essential oils and their carrier oil? If you have a tired Throat chakra, make use of lemon oil. If you need to calm this chakra, try a little vanilla or Roman chamomile. To keep this chakra well maintained, try a little coriander seed oil.

Third Eye Chakra

Many of you may recognize the oil best suited for this chakra: Sandalwood. With its pleasant aroma, this is a great scent to meditate to. It helps with any spiritual journey you may want to undertake and can also help you become the person who you perceive yourself to be.

If a facial massage is not something you enjoy, then dabbing a small amount of oil on your forehead is good enough. Rosemary is a great oil to wake that sleepy Third Eye while German chamomile will calm it and bring it into focus. Frankincense is an excellent oil to help you maintain a healthy Third Eye chakra.

Crown Chakra

If you need an extra boost to help you connect with the immaterial world, lime essential oil is the way to go. If you find that you are often confused about dealing with a situation, this oil helps to clear your mind and allow you to make quick decisions. Like the Third Eye chakra, Frankincense is another great oil (to maintain a balanced chakra) if you do not mind the Christmas flashbacks.

Massaging this chakra is not possible, so try surrounding yourself with the scents with a diffuser. Oils such as spicy-sweet lavender raises the energy in a sluggish Crown chakra whilst neroli or vanilla can add a calming effect.

Please do not limit yourself with just using essential oils to help you achieve what you are trying to do. If you want to tackle a specific problem and not just a chakra, why not consider some living plants if you are not a fan of essential oils or struggle to make your own? Many plants have a strong smell that can also help you concentrate and quite a few are easy to grow in your home. Plants like mint, lemongrass, and lavender can be kept fresh or dried in your home and provide calming scents through your living space.

"Do I need to stick to a single oil or can I blend my own?" Many places online offer their own custom blends under their own names but nothing stops you from making your own blends if you want to create your own unique scent. Montes (2015) suggests a blend of rose geranium, basil, and sandalwood that should be diffused into the air to help with stress. Though a warning should be noted here about allergens. Please make sure that the oils you use can be blended together in such a way that they do not cause adverse reactions to you when you use them. Another thing to note are the names of oils. Do not confuse bitter orange (*Citrus aurantium*) and sweet orange (*C. sinensis*) as the same thing. They are two different species of orange. It is strongly suggested that you do some research into which oils are the ones you need and then making sure to check the name before purchasing it.

"Lastly, how do I know that the oil I am buying is the real deal? I mean, it's not regulated by the FDA, right?" It is true that essential oils are not regulated by the FDA and this is where you will need to have eagle eye vision (or the sense of smell of a dog) to root out the fakes from the true gems (Farr, 2020). If you are buying essential oils there are a few things that need to be noted. When we compared the bitter and sweet oranges you may have noticed those two names in italics that followed. These are the Latin names of the plants and they are crucial. Things to note somewhere on the label of the essential oil bottle is that the common name (sweet orange) is followed by the Latin name (*Citrus sinensis* or *C. sinensis*), if this is not there it is likely fake. If the label simply says essence oil or fragrance oil it is NOT an essential oil. If the label cannot tell you from what part of the plant the oil is made from do not believe that it is an essential oil. If there is an ingredients list then know that this oil has been blended with something else and it is not a true essential oil. Essential oil should only have one ingredient, the essential oil. Look for how the oil was extracted, simply noting cold press or steam distillation is enough to let you know it is the real deal. Finally, the bottle type, essential oils are almost exclusively sold in small brown or amber bottles (sometimes green as in Fig. 9), if this is not the case, it is best to move on and keep looking. Your first defense against snake oil salespeople is being educated enough to spot a fake. Happy shopping!

Fig. 9. Lemongrass essential oil.

Chapter 7:
Chakras, Reiki, Reflexology, and Acupuncture

Up to this point, we have covered a wide variety of holistic methods to healing our chakras from meditation and yoga to crystals and essential oils. These are just but a few of the methods outside of medical practices (alternative medicines) but they are not all of them. In this chapter we will deal with three of those most common of the holistic healing methods.

Overview of Reiki

Reiki is a fairly new practice, late nineteenth century to early twentieth century, when compared to the practices of yoga and meditation. It was developed in

Japan by Dr. Mikao Usui (IARP, n.d.) whose aim was to create a method of healing that was not aligned to any particular religion or belief so that it could benefit all of man. This method of healing was meant to be done through the laying of one's hands upon another and channeling energy—called life force energy or Qi —into the receiver's body. Dr. Usui was always interested in many things and constantly traveled to learn about them but it wasn't until he completed a spiritual journey upon Mount Kurama, which took him 21 days, for Usui Reki to be born.

After this spiritual awakening, he established his clinic for healing and teaching of Reiki in Kyoto, where he became quite well known for his healing practice. Upon his death, he had taught his methods to several Reiki Masters to ensure that what he had learned would not be forgotten. One of those Masters was Dr. Chujiro Hayashi, who went on to develop the Reiki system even more by adding certain hand positions to be able to spread the healing through the whole body more efficiently. He is also credited with improving the attunement process (helping people get ready to use Reiki on themselves or others) of his students. Because of this he was also able to train many more Reiki Masters.

Patient turned Master, Hawayo Takata, a Japanese-American woman, first approached Dr. Hayashi for several health problems she had. Though skeptical of the system, she was willing to try anything to help with the problems she faced. After a few months of treatment, she found that her health problems had been alleviated. She felt that she had to share this wonder with the rest of the world. She was credited with spreading Usui Reiki to America. During her time of training she produced 22 Masters under her.

Reiki still persists today as it is a great tool to reduce stress and aid relaxation. Reiki is not a cure to disease but does assist the body to create an environment that can be beneficial to healing. Because of this, you find that Reiki is practiced with other traditional medical practices and some hospitals even have their own Reiki practitioners.

The important thing to remember with Reiki is that your own energy needs to be clear and filled with good intent before laying hands upon someone else. Reiki can be performed by touching the patient or from a short distance with hand symbols and prayers. There are three levels of Reiki (Langlais, 2020). Level one is aimed to attune a student to using Reiki on themselves and others. Level two concentrates on opening practitioners' Heart chakras whilst they themselves get the ability to open their client's energy channels more. They are also taught the five Reiki symbols, which will help them heal people from a distance. Level three is also known as the Master level. The attunement received here allows the practitioner to attune new students in the art of Reiki, though this is not a requirement.

Benefits of Reiki to Your Chakras

Remember what was said at the beginning of the book? Chakras are nodes which are connected with energy channels. If these nodes are blocked, a Reiki practitioner is able to unblock these chakras by aiding the flow of energy through the body. They do this by slowly hovering their hands over the patient until they locate the blocked chakra, then they use Qi (Alcantara, 2020) to move the blockage and clear the energy channels. Once the energy is flowing more freely the patient should start feeling better, though sessions can vary in number depending on how much work needs to be done.

Overview of Reflexology

People who study Reflexology believe that the various stresses in our lives cause blockages in our vital life force. These blockages cause imbalances and thus lead to many different illnesses (Cirino, 2018). The study of Reflexology (similar to a massage) concentrates on using pressure points in the hands, feet, and ears to help alleviate some of these illnesses. It is believed that these pressure points correspond with different parts of the body. There are even maps of these places that Reflexology practitioners use to help their clients. It is believed that through this touch, the blockages are removed and the flow of life force is restored.

Though Reflexology has shown many benefits, very few of these have actually been evaluated by scientific means. Despite this, improvements have been noted in terms of anxiety and stress, all the way through to pain management in arthritis patients.

However, is this method safe for all to use? Sadly, no. People with certain conditions are warned off of making use of Reflexology. These conditions include gout, ulcers to the hands or feet, or even fungal infections to the areas that the practitioner may have to touch. It is considered a good idea to talk to your doctor before seeking the assistance of a Reflexologist. Pregnancy is also a condition that you need to be very wary of when trying Reflexology, as labor can be triggered by pressing on certain pressure points. If inducing your labor is what you want, please discuss this with your midwife or doctor before going to see a Reflexologist.

This practice was used by the Chinese and Indians, often used with acupuncture, and dates back to 3000 BCE (Ernst & Köder, 1997). The massage developed for Reflexology involves feeling for crystal-like structures (as small as a grain of fine sugar or as big as a grain of regular sugar) or places of sensitivity in the area of study. Physical blockages from these crystals (likely uric acid or calcium crystals) are thought to come from the organ that is malfunctioning and blocks the nerve endings and lymph flow. A precise massage to these areas breaks up the crystal structures, allowing the body to reabsorb them with no negative effects to your body. The act of massaging also promotes an increase of blood flow to the area, which helps move waste products such as lactic acid from the affected area.

Reflexology is not regulated in the USA (Wong, 2019), so if you are looking for a professional, consider making use of someone who is certified from the American Reflexology Certification Board with at least 200 hours of training at a recognized institution.

Benefits of Reflexology to Your Chakras

Body

Reflexology and chakras go quite well together, as the areas of the chakras are often reflected on the maps which practitioners use in their practice of the art. First the problem is identified. For example, with a Root chakra blockage the practitioner will focus on the area of the hand, foot, or ear that corresponds with the chakra (Lui, 2016). Energy is added to those places to help with the blockages and promote the flow of energy through the body once more.

Generally, the practitioner will use thumbs and forefingers to work these areas. With the blockages clear, the body can benefit from the experience and not just the individual limb.

Feet

When looking at a foot, which is placed heel down, the area of your seven main chakras can be mapped as follows (Zollicoffer, n.d.). The Root chakra can be located on the heel and is associated with the sciatic nerve in Reflexology. The Sacral chakra is just under the ankle (inside and outside of the foot) and is associated with the ovaries and testes (outer foot) and uterus and prostate (inner foot). The Solar Plexus chakra is located just under the ball of your foot and is associated with your pancreas and the physical solar plexus, where our diaphragm is found. The Heart chakra is found in the middle of the ball of your foot, just under your second toe and is associated with your heart. If you move your thumb to just under your big toe, you will find the area that is associated with the thymus gland. The Throat chakra is located in the bend of your big toe and is associated with the thyroid gland. The Third Eye chakra is found halfway between the base of your big toe and the tip of it. It is associated with the pituitary gland. The final chakra, the Crown, is found at the very tip of your big toe and is associated with your pineal gland. Everyone loves a good foot rub, so why not try this to help with the flow of your energy through your chakras. Don't forget to work on both feet!

Hands

Some people are not comfortable with having their feet touched and that's okay, as your hands also have your chakras mapped out onto them (AngeLife, 2018). When one looks at the palm of your hand, most of the chakras are mapped along the thumb but some can be found in the palm as well. The Root chakra can be found at the base where your thumb meets your wrist. The Sacral chakra can be found either at the base of your little finger (pinkie) or is half way up the first thumb bone but before the first joint. The Solar Plexus chakra is just in front of the Sacral chakra, but not quite at the first joint. It can also be found in the palm of your hand on the finger joint of the middle finger. The Heart chakra can be found on the first joint of the thumb, as well as the bend of the middle finger where it joins your hand. The Throat chakra can be found on either side of the thumb. The inner side is on the first joint and the second is just above it. The Third Eye chakra is also on both sides of the thumb. On the inside, it is just below the second joint and on the outside, just above. The Crown chakra is at the tip of the thumb and can be held by squeezing from the inner and outer part of the thumb. Treat both hands as you treat both feet.

Overview of Acupuncture

This is another ancient practice that comes from China and was developed ~2500 years ago. The technique, using thin, sharp needles, were used to manipulate the flow of a patient's Qi if it wasn't flowing the way it was supposed to (Stern, n.d.). According to acupuncture theory there are 12 meridians (conduits) in the body that corresponds with the body's main organs (heart, etc.). Very much like chakras, the meridians can be blocked or have a deficiency of energy that needs to be cleared. Each meridian has its own symptoms depending on whether it has a deficiency of energy or if it is blocked by excess energy.

Why does acupuncture work? Well, those of the west believe that upon insertion of the needles, the brain reacts by releasing a chemical compound called serotonin. This is a vital chemical in our bodies as it helps with many things including getting that good night's rest by regulating your sleep patterns.

"Acupuncture uses needles so it hurts a lot right, kind of like getting a tattoo?" Not at all! These needles are very thin and sharp so you should only really feel a slight pinch as the needle is inserted. The practice is meant to be painless if done correctly. If you feel pain during an acupuncture session, you need to tell the practitioner so that they can re-evaluate how to treat you.

What does acupuncture treat? Mostly acupuncture is used to treat a wide range of pains but can also be used to treat other illnesses like insomnia.

When one goes to an acupuncture appointment, depending on the problem, you may be asked to remove the clothes from that area and told to lie down and relax. Needles are added to depths from 0.5 to 8 cm and in a pattern that would be most beneficial to the flow of Qi (Helms, n.d.). Usually only a specific area is targeted for energy flow. If multiple areas are affected, several sessions may be needed to clear all meridians. Sometimes the acupuncture practitioner will add heat, pressure, or even electricity (low-frequency, high stimulation of 2 to 4 Hz or even high frequency, low intensity of 70 Hz or more) to the needles whilst they are embedded. If you have been treated with acupuncture in conjunction with electricity, you will know exactly how strange it feels.

Acupuncture can be combined with other medical practices such as physiotherapy or even holistic medicine such as Reflexology. It is still strongly suggested that you talk to your doctor before trying any new treatment for any existing medical conditions you may have.

If you are seeking an acupuncturist it is a good idea to contact the American Academy of Medical Acupuncture. They are fairly strict with their entrance requirement of a full time practitioner. The practitioner will need to complete no less than 220 hours of formal training and at least two years of clinical experience before being accepted.

As this technique uses needles that can go various depths in the body, please be aware of possible side effects when making use of this healing process. Bleeding and bruising is fairly normal but internal bleeding is not, so make sure you are seeing a professional. A professional will never use the same needle twice. Once used, the needles need to be disposed of to prevent the spread of diseases like Hepatitis. Some people have noted pain or feeling exhausted after the treatment. If pain persists, please contact your practitioner for further steps that need to be taken.

Benefits of Acupuncture to Your Chakras

The *point* of acupuncture (get it?) is to move the life force through the body more efficiently. If this energy is misaligned or blocked, the act of adding the needles to the right positions on the body is important to our overall health and not just pain management (Amaro, 2003). Each chakra is represented by a specific location on the body. The Root chakra is found in position Ren-1 (Conception Vessel 1), which is found in the center perineum (Clogstoun-Willmott, 2020e), however, most practitioners would rather use Kidney-1 to treat this chakra. The Sacral chakra is found at position Ren 3-8 (Conception Vessel 3), which is just above the pelvic bone if you draw a line towards your belly (not to be used if a woman is pregnant) (Clogstoun-Willmott, 2020a). The Solar Plexus chakra is found in position Ren-12, which is just under the last set of ribs (Clogstoun-Willmott, 2020b). The Heart chakra is found at Ren-17, which is in the middle of your chest (Clogstoun-Willmott, 2020d). The Throat chakra is found at Ren-22, which is just under your thyroid (Clogstoun-Willmott, 2020c). The Third Eye chakra is found at Yin Tang, which is between your two eyebrows (Brown, 2014). The Crown chakra is found at DU-20 (also known as the Governor Vessel 20), which is in the middle of the top of your head (Larsen, 2016). The sites mentioned are just some of the sites that can be used for clearing your chakra and aiding in healing from many issues.

Reiki, Reflexology, and acupuncture are by no means the only options you have when it comes to realigning your chakras to where you want them to be. There are several other alternative healings you can try if you are curious. Something that is quite popular nowadays is Homeopathy. This practice was developed in Germany and uses the doctrine of "like cures like." It is the belief of these practitioners that if the herbs and natural medicines they use cause the symptoms of the disease in a healthy person, it can be given to the sick person in small doses to aid in self-healing of the body (Khare, 2017). Naturopathy is another practice that heals through natural means (herbalism, reflexology, etc.) to aid self-healing. Acupressure is very similar to acupuncture, if you have a fear of needles that you just cannot get over why not try this healing therapy? Instead of needles, the practitioner uses their hands and even elbows to reach the places on your body that need the attention. Ayurveda is a practice from India which teaches harmony with nature and self-healing. This healing therapy makes use of herbal medicine, breathing techniques, as well as meditation and yoga.

During the chapter of yoga, it was mentioned that when sitting in the Easy Pose your thumb and index finger need to be touching. Yoga and meditation can be accompanied by another practice called Mundra. Mundras are special hand positions (Rice, 2020), each having their own special meaning, which can be used to represent many things. The seven main chakras have their own hand positions. The Root chakra uses the muladhara mudra, the Sacral chakra uses the shakti mudra, the Solar Plexus chakra uses the rudra mudra, the Heart chakra uses the padma mudra, the Throat chakra uses the granthita mudra, the Third Eye uses the mudra of the great head and lastly, the Crown chakra uses the mudra of a thousand petals and is above your head.

At the end of the day you will need to decide what you want from these therapies, what you are willing to put in and if you are able to finish what you start. All of this will take time and there are no shortcuts. There are no cure-alls irrespective of the medicine you use, be it conventional or alternative. On a final note, it is very important to discuss any alternative therapies with your doctor before you attempt them.

Chapter 8:
Safe for the Whole Family?

That is quite an interesting question to ask and in essence, yes. Working with chakras is something that is fairly safe to do. It is important to note, especially if you want to do chakra work with children, that chakras develop and rule over our lives at different periods of our existence. According to Meulman (2012), the Root chakra develops during the first six months of our life, while the Sacral chakra develops between six months and two years. The Solar plexus chakra develops between two and four years and the Heart chakra develops between four and seven years. The Throat chakra develops between seven and twelve years of life and between twelve and eighteen (teenage stage), the Third Eye chakra develops. The last of the chakras to fully develop and mature is the Crown chakra, and it happens between your last year of being a teenager until your death (implying you work on it continually). During the full development of these chakras, our life enters cycles of seven years which is also ruled by the various chakras. According to Krstevska (n.d.), the cycles are as follows: Root chakra (1-7 years), Sacral chakra (8-14), Solar Plexus chakra (15-21), Heart chakra (22-28), Throat chakra (29-35), Third Eye chakra (36-42) and Crown chakra (43-49). Each cycle corresponds with what we are meant to learn during this time, for example, the Heart cycle is where we learn to truly love ourselves and those around us.

Do Animals Have Chakras?

Chakras govern all stages of our lives from birth to death, but are humans the only creatures that have chakras? Not a chance! Anything that lives has a form of energy that moves through it. Think of that furry little one that is sitting on your lap or at your feet, or perhaps the feathered one sleeping in their cage. They are all included in that list.

Differences Between People and Animals

The Earth is bountiful in life, humans only make up a small portion of life that exists on it. Humans make up no more that 0.01% of biomass (organic mass) on our planet and only 2.5% of all the animal biomass (Ritchie, 2019). It stands to reason that we would share some kind of similarity with our animal brethren. That becomes quite clear when we look at our chakras. We share our seven main chakras but animals have one more main one than us. The Brachial chakra, discovered by Margrit Coates (Gehi 2016), is special to animals and can be found on both sides of the body in the area of the shoulders. Where in humans the central chakra is considered the Heart chakra, the Brachial chakra is the center for the animals. If an animal is in need of spiritual healing, it should start here. Other chakras to note here are the Bud chakras, which can be found in the feet and on either side of the ear on the skull, and the Sensory chakras, which are in positions where the animal gathers sensory data. The other difference in the chakras is that animals have not one, but two areas for the Heart chakra (the second one is known as alternative Heart chakra) (Patinkas, n.d.).

The Brachial chakra is not only important for the animal, but also for the relationship they could possibly forge with us. If we are struggling to bond with an animal it is likely because the Brachial is weak or blocked, which can cause the animal not to want to connect with anyone and sometimes will also avoid being touched. This chakra is what links all other chakras in the animal.

Do animals also suffer imbalances in their other chakras? Sadly, yes they do, and each chakra has its

119

own symptoms (Patinkas, n.d. & Natural Chakra Healing n.d.). A Root chakra (base of the tail) that is unbalanced causes the animal to enter a flight mode where they are extremely scared with no cause. Another side effect is that the animal becomes greedy with their food and this can lead to obesity. Other physical problems that can manifest include constipation and problems with the lower limbs or paws. To help your pet heal, spend time with them outdoors doing activities like walking or running. If your pet, or you, are not up for long walks or runs, consider lying outside and just enjoy watching the clouds float by.

If a Sacral chakra (lower back) is unbalanced, the animal may whine more than normal with no apparent cause and have boundary issues. Working animals (horse or dogs, as an example) may find it difficult to distinguish between work time and play time. Physical problems that can manifest here include bladder and back problems. Healing can be as simple as bathing your pet, if they are not afraid of water. If your companion is afraid of bathing, why not take a walk around a body of water to cleanse this chakra?

An unbalanced Solar Plexus chakra (middle of the back) causes several confusing behaviors such as aggression, acts of dominance, being withdrawn, or showing no enthusiasm in anything. Physical problems that occur include eating disorders and poor digestion. You can meditate with your furry companion if they are calm (be wary if you like to put essential oils on any surface as they might want to lick it and can get sick) or a simple belly rub can aid the healing in this chakra.

A Heart chakra (extends from chest to behind the forelegs) that is unbalanced causes an animal to be sad, showing possessive (jealous) behavior, or just simply refuses to interact with any other animal. The heart is the main organ that is affected if this chakra is unbalanced. To help balance this chakra, send your loving intent to your pet. Show love by spending time with the animal be it furry, feathered, or scaly.

An unbalanced Throat chakra (length of the throat, though with longer throated animals it can be found over the vocal cords) causes a normally quiet animal to become excessively noisy and a talkative animal to become silent. Animals who have been trained to obey commands will suddenly no longer listen to them. To help with this chakra, consider playing some music and singing or humming around your pet. You will need to experiment with what music your companion may like. Everyone has their favorite and so will they.

What we know as the Third Eye chakra is called the Brow chakra in animals (center of the head, above the eyes). If this chakra is unbalanced, the animal can show signs of a headache, poor eyesight, or will be distracted by everything, unable to remain focused. Other physical problems that can occur are problems with balance and coordination. Healing with crystals, meditation, and guided visualizations of your pet being healed is the way to go if you want this chakra to realign.

If the Crown chakra (top of the head) is unbalanced, the animal will appear withdrawn, depressed, and lethargic. This chakra can be realigned the same way as the Brow chakra.

If the Brachial chakra (aka the Key chakra) is unbalanced, the animal will fear any contact with humans and avoid them as much as possible. If they cannot escape and feel cornered, they may turn aggressive and hostile (as any animal will when feeling threatened). If this is the case with an animal you come across in the street please DO NOT approach by yourself, rather, contact professionals who can catch the animal in a manner that is safe for everyone and every animal involved. It sounds pretty grim but this chakra can be balanced though hands-on healing and distant reiki healing. A damaged Brachial chakra requires a lot of hard work and time, as you will need to earn the animal's trust again. Slowly take steps to show that you can be trusted and increase the amount of love that you show to the animal until you are able to touch it and physically share your love with it.

How can an animal's chakras be realigned? In a similar fashion with how we balance ours with gemstones. In fact, the seven main chakras of an animal are balanced with the same kinds of gemstones. The

Brachial chakra (associated with the color black) that causes an animal to be reluctant to connect can be aided with the use of a black tourmaline or a clear quartz crystal that has been powered with selfless intentions (a powered quartz) for the animal. This is not the only healing that is available to your pets (House of Healing, n.d.). Reiki also offers beneficial treatment to them. This practice can help your pet through mental anguish, such as losing a friend or owner, that could result in pining. It can also assist with nervous rescue pets as well as initial first aid care for an animal on the way to the vet to keep it calm (Canines of Mind, n.d.).

Visualizing is also a great way to help you heal a pet with imbalanced chakras and the great thing is that you can do it from a distance (McKenzie, 2019). Think of the times you have been forced to leave your pet overnight at the vet. You are always so worried, but instead of feeling the worriedness, rather, change the way you think and concentrate on sending white healing energy to your furry companion. Imagine that it surrounds them as it aids them in the process of healing.

Margrit Coates (Coates, n.d.) has a very powerful message about healing animals with techniques that have to do with lay on hand practices. This healing should not be a replacement for veterinary care. Just like this book suggests that you seek medical assistance before trying alternative therapies, it even more strongly suggests seeing a vet for a sick animal before trying alternative means of healing. Remember, your pet relies on you to make decisions for its health, safety, and security. It is unable to see to its own medical care. You will need to make these decisions. Speak to a professional first before making a decision.

Helping a New Pet Bond Through Chakras

Very few people have had the absolute pleasure of walking into a shelter or pet store and just knowing which animal in there was for you. Even fewer have had the honor of being chosen by an animal. Staring into a cage and a rat leaps at you with a quivering nose and huge eyes begging to come home with you. That shy cat that never managed to be adopted suddenly comes to life as you walk into the room. The abused and broken dog that has no social skills suddenly has a tail wag when it lays its eyes on you. If you search for the term heart animal on pet forums, you will find people often use this to describe an animal that has had a special bond with them from the second they laid eyes upon them. Sadly, not everyone has this joyous experience and you have to actually work hard and spend a lot of time to earn the trust of the animal you are bringing into your life.

Maclennan (2016) has some excellent pointers when it comes to bonding with your pet. The first thing to remember is that bonding does take time, it doesn't occur overnight. The Brachial chakra that was discussed earlier is momentous in the bonding process. We connect with our pets on an energy level through this chakra. If this chakra is blocked (sadly due to many things) or is weak, bonding may be difficult and if no results are forthcoming, you can get help with animal therapists or trainers that could give you more in-depth advice.

However, if you aren't quite ready to make use of an animal therapist, take the time to really sit down with your pet. The emotional center of humans is our Heart chakra, so if you have a pet which is not averse to being held, sit with them on or near your chest. This is highly dependent on the size of your pet! This book does not recommend cuddling a horse on your couch. Unless you want to. It's not like we can stop you.

If closeness is not possible (aggression or nervousness in the animal), show your good intentions to the animal by making its environment comfortable (food, shelter, etc.) and give the animal space. You don't like it if someone keeps asking you every five minutes if you're okay, so leave your pet to adjust. It will take time, but the animal will come around. Be ready for that stare around the door or the start of a wag in the tail.

If the animal doesn't like cuddles but doesn't mind touch, why not consider long strokes along the back and flanks? If you can target the Brachial chakra, that would be best. Remember that your Heart chakra also has a position along your thumb, so make sure you use your full hand to pet the animal. Long, gentle strokes are all it takes and a total 100% of dogs that read this book would agree that being pet is the best.

Lastly, your intent needs to be clear. If you intend to love and care for this animal it will know and eventually bond. Try not to raise your voice, show nervousness, or frustration. Animals are able to pick up on that and bonding will take longer.

Only for Common Pets? Not at All!

Whilst gathering knowledge for this chapter of the book it was noted that many charts that map animal chakras are available quite freely on the internet. Though the animals which are quite often represented in these charts are our common furry friends, the cat and dog. That being said, it was also noted that larger animals like the horse have also been mapped. Now there is likely a cry from several (hundred?) people demanding to know about fish or birds or rodents. Surely even these little guys have some kind of chakra system that we can use to help them feel better if they are down as they make us feel good about ourselves? The short answer is yes, all life has some form of chakra system to it. Above we mentioned the locations of the eight main chakras of the animals. If you are patient, you will be able to gently test out where each one is on your smaller, more exotic pets. As for snakes, well, a lot of patience may be needed for this.

Hedgehogs, Rabbits, and Rats, Oh My!

This section is a bit of a thought experiment (give it a try and see how it goes) where three exotic pets have been chosen to try and work out how we can bond with them. Let's start with the rabbit. The rabbit is a prey animal (which means in its development it was hunted as food). An animal like this is not the kind that would bond easily to someone who moves fast or grabs at them. Bonding with a rabbit starts from afar. Make a comfortable hutch with plenty of food, shelter, and water. You have to fill this space with your intent to care and love this animal. Once it is more comfortable with its space you can move onto making it comfortable with your presence. Be slow and steady, offering food from your hand. You may get a sniff and a hop away or you can be rewarded with a nibble taken from your hand. Sit and talk with it, show your intent to bond. In time, the animal will hop to the edge of its hutch to investigate and you can attempt to pet it. Remember that Brachial chakra? Gently run some fingers over this place and see how your animal reacts. If it hasn't scampered away yet, try slowly rubbing your hand down their back. There is the start of a beautiful friendship. Do be careful of carrying your rabbits, as they can be spooked by things outside of your control and they will jump and run to seek shelter.

Rats. Vermin. Plague bearers. Negative thoughts like that will never get you to bond with a very intelligent animal that is so curious about the world. Rats, like rabbits, are prey animals, so gaining their trust can be tricky as they will not hesitate to bite if they feel threatened. Similarly to a rabbit, you need the right environment for the rat to feel comfortable and stimulated in. The way to a rat's heart is its stomach. Treats like fruit or rat blocks are a great way for you to entice your little friend to come and sniff your hand. If you are lucky and you got a friendly little one, you will often be rewarded with a lick to show friendship. Pet gently between the shoulder blades towards the sides. Try to avoid the tail at first, as not all rats are comfortable with this interaction. Allow the rat to explore you and soon you will have a little buddy riding on your shoulders or inside your hoodie pouch.

Hedgehogs (Fig. 10). Oh boy, here is an extreme case. How do we even access any of the chakras in that spiny creature? Spend some time on sites like YouTube and you will see that these guys are notorious grumps! This does not mean that you cannot bond with your little spiny creature. Almost all the chakras are covered in spines if the animal is stressed. Here your intent needs to be very clear from

128

the start. A good home, understanding their nature (nocturnal) and time. There is nothing quite like having a hedgehog uncurl close to you, look around, see you, waddle to you, and then lie down on you with its belly as close to you as possible. When a hedgehog willingly lies flat on you it shares all its chakras with you. This is one animal that you cannot force love upon. It will show its love and intent if you continue to share your energy through your intent to it.

Fig. 10. Curious hedgehog.

Conclusion

So, what is our take home message from all of this? Everything around us is governed by energies which our bodies make use of to exist. If we find ourselves in a negative situation, stressful work environment, assault, etc., our energies are negatively affected by this. Our own personal energies (chakras) are in different places throughout our bodies. Each chakra can become unbalanced due to external forces and it is upon us to try and correct them as best as possible. Our mindset also needs to change if we want to change our own intent for our lives. Positive thinking and positive actions will cause our chakras to improve, thus making our lives and health improve too. Chakras can be balanced in many different ways, some discussed in this book and some are left for you to explore on your own. At the end of the day, you are the one that needs to be comfortable with the way your own energies feel in your body. Time is something that you need to take to look into yourself and find out what is causing your imbalance. This healing takes a while but it is possible, one step at a time.

The study of chakras and the various holistic methods used to balance them are almost as old as time. Somewhere, something is working, or this would not have continued developing in a modern world with medicine and other technologies which are at our disposal. This book does not recommend that the therapies that it shares (for animals and humans alike) replace the advice and guidance of a doctor or veterinary surgeon, it seeks to be therapeutic and to aid in healing and growth of ourselves. Only you can decide what is right for you. Be it yoga, meditation, or even the use of crystals. Anything to help with the stressful existence of the physical world. If you are able to find the calm that alludes most people, then you have already taken a step forward in your own self-healing. If you are able to find peace, then this book has done its job. When you find that perfect balance for your chakras, don't forget that it is an ongoing process to keep them balanced, either through grounding the overexcited nodes or boosting the weak or sluggish ones. You cannot assume that they will remain balanced. Small changes in your everyday life can mean the difference between a quick five-minute yoga session or having to go see a Reiki Master to help you with more serious problems.

You do not have to take this journey on your own. Consider working together with a friend or even your pet to aid in your healing or theirs. This book is but a guideline as to what you can do to self-heal. It is strongly suggested that you do your own research and come to your own conclusion about the various alternative therapies that are available to you where you live.

Other Books by Judith Yandell

Do You Want To Free Yourself From Stress And Anxiety? Would you like to bring peace and joy in your life?

Many people hear the word "Buddhism" and they think it is a religion. However, a person of any religion can bring Buddhist principles into their life without giving up their religious beliefs.

Buddhism is a simple and practical philosophy, practiced by more than 300 million people worldwide, that can make your life better and help you find inner peace and happiness.

Buddhism is a way of living your life following a path of spiritual development that leads you to the truth of reality.

"We are shaped by our thoughts; we become what we think. When the mind is pure, joy follows like a shadow that never leaves." - Buddha

Nowadays, Buddhism is becoming increasingly popular, thanks to the positive benefits it can bring to those who choose to practice it.

By following the principles of Buddhism and by practicing mindfulness meditation you can reduce anxiety and stress and bring clarity and joy into your mind.

If you want to learn how to apply the Buddhist philosophy in your everyday life, then this book is for you.

You'll learn the principles of this philosophy along with the history of Buddha and his teachings that will help you successfully bring Buddhism into your everyday life.

This book will give you the answers you're seeking in a format that is both simple and easy to understand, without obscure words or convoluted sentences.

Inside Buddhism for Beginners, discover:

- How you can bring peace and joy in your life following the simple principles of Buddhism

- A simple but effective meditation technique for beginners to help you relieve stress and feel calmer, even if you've never meditated before
- The core Buddhist principles and teachings explained in plain english, without complex or obscure words
- The History of Buddhism, from its origins to the present day
- Why knowing and freeing your mind can help you bring peace and joy in your everyday life (with practical tips to help you start)
- A complete historical timeline of notable buddhist events to help you understand the development of this philosophy
- The principles you should pursue if you want to follow the path of Buddha
- An effective way to understand and practice Buddhism without feeling overwhelmed
- The truth about Karma and how it can actually help you change your life (many people don't know this)
- Practical tips to bring Buddhism into your everyday life and brighten your future.

And much, much more. Now it's up to you. Even if right now you have no clue of Buddha's teachings, let joy and peace become part of your life and free you from stress and anxiety, you won't regret it!

"Buddhism for Beginners" by Judith Yandell is available at Amazon.

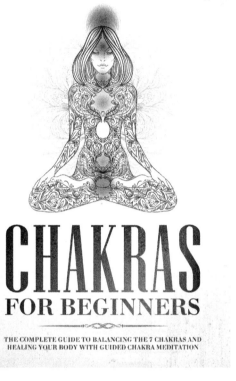

JUDITH YANDELL

CHAKRAS
FOR BEGINNERS

THE COMPLETE GUIDE TO BALANCING THE 7 CHAKRAS AND
HEALING YOUR BODY WITH GUIDED CHAKRA MEDITATION

If you want to learn how to awaken and balance your chakras to bring joy and harmony in your life, then keep reading...

You might have a problem with your chakras without even realizing it. Do you experience headaches, neck pain or sore throat? Do you feel ill and emotionally unstable at times? Do you have troubles making decisions or feel lost and without a purpose in life? These are just a few signs of unbalanced chakras.

If you experience any of these symptoms, I want you

to know that there's a solution. You see, the 7 chakras are the energy centers of your body. If they're blocked or out of balance, you'll feel the repercussions in your body. If you want to reap the benefits of a healthier mind and bring harmony in your life, you have to balance your chakras and unlock their power.

Inside Chakras for Beginners, discover:
• How you can balance your chakras and heal your energy system to bring balance into your life
• What are the 7 chakras and how do they work
• The locations and functions of the 7 chakras, from Root to Crown
• 5 lessons for clearing chakra blockages and bringing harmony and balance in your life
• How damaged chakras are affecting your life and how you can heal them (many people don't even know they have chakra blockages)
• Lists of questions to help you concentrate on the specific energy of each chakra and balance each one more effectively.
• Why balancing chakras is important and why everyone should be doing it.
• Helpful techniques and practices to keep your chakras open
• Useful strategies to bring harmony and balance in your life.
• Kundalini techniques and practices to awaken your chakras
• The most common issues created by a clogged chakra system and how to solve them
• 7 effective meditations, one for each chakra, to help you clear energy blockages and enhance your life

And much, much more!

Even if you have zero knowledge about chakras and energetic balance, this beginner's guide will help you clear your whole chakra system and live your life in harmony and balance. The truth is, when you learn how to activate and clear your chakras, they will let positive energy flow to every part of your body, mind and spirit. So, if you want to heal your body and spirit and balance your chakras to bring joy and wellness into your life, grab your copy now.

**"Chakras for Beginners" by Judith Yandell
is available at Amazon.**

EMPATH

SURVIVAL AND HEALING GUIDE FOR
EMPATHS AND HIGHLY SENSITIVE PEOPLE
TO SHIELD YOURSELF FROM NEGATIVE ENERGIES,
MANAGE YOUR EMPATHY AND DEVELOP YOUR GIFT

JUDITH YANDELL

We all feel some kind of empathy towards others. But if you have no control over your empathy and always have the obsession of fixing other people, then you know how painfully frustrating being an empath is.

Empaths are usually overwhelmed by other people's emotions, they feel what others feel and are able to profoundly understand their mind. As a result, empaths care for everyone else but themselves. They become "magnets" for negative people that want to take advantage of the empaths' ability to understand opinions and emotions of others.

However, I want you to know that being an empath doesn't have to be so negative. You may have not yet realized it, but you have a powerful and beautiful gift. If you learn how to embrace it and channel your empathy, you can use it for spreading kindness, love and positive energy to the world.

In this book you'll learn:
- 6 Powerful Methods You Can Use to Control Your Gift (Hint: They Don't Include "Avoid Social Situations" and "Lock Yourself Up in You House")
- The Single Most Effective Thing You Can Do to Shield Yourself From Energy Vampires
- 11 Most Common Personality Traits of Empaths
- Powerful Techniques to Develop Your Skills and Channel Your Empathy to Spread Positive Energy
- How To Use a Specific Kind of Negative Thinking to Actually Overcome Your Social Anxiety
- 20 Statements to Help You Determine if You Really Are an Empath
- Is an Energy Vampire Preying on You? Here's How to Find Out
- How to Find Out if Your Child Is an Empath and What You Can Do to Support
- A Positive Affirmations Routine That Can Help You Accept Yourself as an Empath and Strengthen Your Abilities
- How Detoxifying a Certain Area of Your Brain Can Help You Embrace Your Empathic Abilities and Improve Your Sense of Intuition
- Why in Certain Cases Accepting Negativity Can Actually Help You Feel Better.

Even if right now you feel you have no control over your abilities, I want you to know that you can learn how to manage your empathy and develop your gift in the right way.

"Empath" by Judith Yandell
is available at Amazon.

Made in the USA
Middletown, DE
22 November 2020

24757363R00080